DATE DUE

AUG 2	8 1990		

Labor Relations and the Litigation Explosion

ROBERT J. FLANAGAN

The Brookings Institution / Washington, D.C.

Copyright © 1987 by
THE BROOKINGS INSTITUTION
1775 Massachusetts Avenue, N.W., Washington, D.C. 20036

Library of Congress Cataloging-in-Publication data:
Flanagan, Robert J.
  Labor relations and the litigation explosion.
  Includes index.
  1. Labor laws and legislation—United States.
I. Title.
KF3319.F53   1987   344.73'01'0269   87-6404
ISBN 0-8157-2858-1   347.30410269
ISBN 0-8157-2857-3 (pbk.)

9 8 7 6 5 4 3 2 1

THE BROOKINGS INSTITUTION is an independent organization devoted to nonpartisan research, education, and publication in economics, government, foreign policy, and the social sciences generally. Its principal purposes are to aid in the development of sound public policies and to promote public understanding of issues of national importance.

The Institution was founded on December 8, 1927, to merge the activities of the Institute for Government Research, founded in 1916, the Institute of Economics, founded in 1922, and the Robert Brookings Graduate School of Economics and Government, founded in 1924.

The Board of Trustees is responsible for the general administration of the Institution, while the immediate direction of the policies, program, and staff is vested in the President, assisted by an advisory committee of the officers and staff. The by-laws of the Institution state: "It is the function of the Trustees to make possible the conduct of scientific research, and publication, under the most favorable conditions, and to safeguard the independence of the research staff in the pursuit of their studies and in the publication of the results of such studies. It is not a part of their function to determine, control, or influence the conduct of particular investigations or the conclusions reached."

The President bears final responsibility for the decision to publish a manuscript as a Brookings book. In reaching his judgment on the competence, accuracy, and objectivity of each study, the President is advised by the director of the appropriate research program and weighs the views of a panel of expert outside readers who report to him in confidence on the quality of the work. Publication of a work signifies that it is deemed a competent treatment worthy of public consideration but does not imply endorsement of conclusions or recommendations.

The Institution maintains its position of neutrality on issues of public policy in order to safeguard the intellectual freedom of the staff. Hence interpretations or conclusions in Brookings publications should be understood to be solely those of the authors and should not be attributed to the Institution, to its trustees, officers, or other staff members, or to the organizations that support its research.

Foreword

REGULATION of the procedural aspects of labor-management relations is more pervasive in the United States than in any other democratic nation. Under the National Labor Relations Act, workers have the right to join unions and bargain collectively, and both labor and management are required to avoid statutorily defined unfair activities. Ironically, though the NLRA was intended to assist the development of collective bargaining between labor and management, union membership in the private sector has declined notably in recent years. Many observers argue that the regulatory structure set up to encourage collective bargaining now interferes with the rights that the act sought to guarantee and provides significant barriers to unionization. The number of unfair labor practice charges has indeed grown rapidly since the mid-1950s, and there are many signs of increased resistance by employers to unions and collective bargaining. This has led some labor leaders to propose deregulation of labor-management relations—repeal of the National Labor Relations Act.

In this study, Robert J. Flanagan analyzes the nature, causes, and consequences of the litigation explosion that has developed under the National Labor Relations Act. He finds that the growth of unfair labor practice charges cannot be explained by a few key changes in legal doctrine, by the volume of regulated labor relations activity, or by general economic developments. Instead, he shows that labor and management have responded to the changing incentives to comply with and to enforce the NLRA. In particular, Flanagan finds that the sustained rise in the union-nonunion wage differential between 1969 and 1982 has had a more profound effect on union coverage of the work force than the growth of unfair labor practice charges. For that reason, although alternative policies might provide stronger guarantees of rights under the act, they are unlikely to reverse the decline in unionization.

Robert J. Flanagan, who is associate professor of labor economics at the Graduate School of Business, Stanford University, wrote this book while he was a visiting fellow at Brookings. He is grateful to many persons and organizations for their assistance during the preparation of this study. The Office of Statistical Services at the National Labor Relations Board provided much of the data analyzed in the study. Julius G. Getman, Bernard Meltzer, Myron Roomkin, and Paul Weiler offered valuable comments on the study, as did the participants in conferences and seminars at Stanford University, the University of California at Berkeley, and the Trade Union Institute for Economic Research in Stockholm, Sweden. Patricia J. Regan at Brookings and Lori Wilson at Stanford provided careful research assistance, and Susan L. Woollen at Brookings and El Vera Fisher at Stanford typed several revisions of the manuscript. The manuscript was edited by Alice M. Carroll, and its factual content was verified by Almaz Zelleke. Florence Robinson prepared the index. The Graduate School of Business, Stanford University, provided financial support for the project.

The views presented here are those of the author and should not be ascribed to the persons or organizations whose assistance is acknowledged above, or to the trustees, officers, or staff members of the Brookings Institution.

BRUCE K. MACLAURY
President

March 1987
Washington, D.C.

Contents

Tables

Figures

CHAPTER 1

Labor Policy and
Regulatory Litigation

A HALF CENTURY has passed since Congress moved the federal government into the regulation of labor-management relations with the adoption of the National Labor Relations Act (NLRA).[1] This statute, passed in 1935 and amended in 1947 and 1959, established the right of workers to join unions and bargain collectively as a matter of public policy. It supported this right by providing a government-supervised election procedure through which employees could select a union representative and by forbidding certain "unfair labor practices" that were believed to inhibit the basic objectives of the act. The NLRA also established a regulatory agency, the National Labor Relations Board (NLRB), to supervise representation elections and to investigate and adjudicate charges of unfair labor practices.

When the NLRA was passed, it was thought that unfair practices might wither away as unions and collective bargaining gained greater acceptability and as the statute clarified the rules of the game in labor-management relations. Instead, the sheer volume of regulatory litigation has become the most salient feature of labor relations policy. The number of unfair labor practice charges filed by unions, employers, and workers has doubled every decade since the mid-1950s, while the volume of labor relations activities subject to regulation—largely union representation elections and collective bargaining negotiations—has remained stable. While the jurisdiction of the NLRA has expanded, compliance with the act has become a major problem. Yet, the growth of regulatory activity under the U.S. approach to labor relations policy has received little analytical attention despite its potential consequences for the collective

1. National Labor Relations Act, chap. 372, 49 Stat. 449 (1935)(codified as amended at 29 USC 151–69 [1982 and supp. III 1986]).

1

bargaining rights of workers and for union representation. In particular, remarkably little is known about compliance and enforcement decisions made under the NLRA.

This book examines the factors that have contributed to the increase in regulatory litigation and the consequences of the litigation explosion for labor relations. It provides an economic and statistical analysis of the effects of regulatory rule making on labor relations behavior and on the regulatory process and hence differs from legal research into the interpretation of specific doctrines and rules developed by the NLRB. It also discusses the implications of the analysis for the future of regulatory policy under the NLRA.

The effect of regulatory policy under the NLRA has become increasingly controversial, because much has changed in American labor relations since the passage of the act. In the early 1930s American unions were weak and they represented a smaller fraction of workers than their counterparts in Western Europe. The labor movement mainly represented skilled-craft workers—the high-wage elite of the blue-collar work force. Efforts to extend unionization to unskilled and semiskilled workers in the large-scale, mass-production industries that accounted for an increasingly large proportion of employment were met by determined employer resistance that often culminated in strikes and violence.

Over the five decades that unions in the private sector have been covered by the NLRA their economic influence has grown and then declined, although union representation still remains well above the levels of the early 1930s.[2] Successful organizing by new industrial unions extended union representation to manufacturing and other industries in the late 1930s and early 1940s. Public policy, initially one-sided in its support of unionization, shifted against the interests of unions after World War II with the passage of the Taft-Hartley Act (the Labor Management Relations Act, 1947) and the Landrum-Griffin Act (the Labor-Management Reporting and Disclosure Act of 1959), as well as with the failure of a 1977 labor law reform bill favored by unions. The Taft-Hartley amendments of the NLRA define several areas of union conduct as unfair labor practices, provide for the disestablishment of unions through decertification elections, and provide emergency dispute procedures that can be invoked when major labor disputes are believed

2. Since the mid-1960s, unionization among public sector employees has spread substantially. Labor relations in the public sector are regulated by a variety of federal, state, and local legislation not included in this study.

to threaten serious harm to the public at large. The Landrum-Griffin amendments marked a shift in emphasis from the regulation of union-management relations to the regulation of the internal affairs of unions.[3] The 1977 reforms that unions sought would have tightened certain aspects of the administration of the NLRA and provided punitive damages for serious violations of the act.

On the surface, the state of labor relations appears more placid than in the late 1920s and 1930s. Much of the contention in labor relations, however, has shifted from the streets and picket lines to the courts and regulatory hearing rooms. Under the NLRA, union organizing is to an important extent a legal process with an intricate set of rules (established over the years by the NLRB) governing almost every aspect of conduct by unions and employers as they seek to influence how workers vote on the question of unionization. Once a union is established, work stoppages can and do occur in support of collective bargaining demands. Regulations implementing a legal duty to bargain may influence both the conduct and substance of collective bargaining. Another set of regulations is directed at the fairness with which unions represent their members under a collective bargaining agreement. The result has been a level of regulatory activity and litigiousness in labor relations that is without parallel in the rest of the world.[4]

With the growing litigiousness have come diverse criticisms of the law. One group of critics faults the NLRA for reducing competition and economic efficiency in labor markets by facilitating the cartelization of labor supply.[5] They argue that monopsony and other labor market imperfections that the organization of workers into unions is meant to counter are not prevalent enough to justify setting aside the pro-competition thrust of the common law treatment of labor unions and labor relations.

Another group of critics holds that the national policy of encouraging collective bargaining expressed in the NLRA is no longer fulfilled in the administration of the act. Unions and some academic observers attribute

---

3. The Landrum-Griffin Act includes a few amendments to the NLRA, but its main thrust is the regulation of internal union affairs, which has little bearing on this study.

4. This appears to be true even in comparison to regulatory systems that share many features of the NLRA. See comparisons with Canada and Japan in chap. 3.

5. Richard A. Epstein, "A Common Law for Labor Relations: A Critique of the New Deal Labor Legislation," *Yale Law Journal*, vol. 92 (July 1983), pp. 1357–1408; Richard A. Posner, "Some Economics of Labor Law," *University of Chicago Law Review*, vol. 51 (Fall 1984), pp. 988–1011.

much of the decline in the unionization of workers in the private sector to employer resistance and argue that the present rules and procedures of the NLRB do more to protect the rights of employers than to guarantee workers' right to select unions without coercion.[6] They contend that the law has fallen short of its goals because too much weight has been given in its implementation to exactly those interests that proponents of the common law wish to protect.[7] Proposals for reform in the administration of the act range from speeding up case processing and imposing more stringent penalties for violations of the act to complete deregulation—abolishing the NLRA—on the grounds that the act currently places more restrictions on the tactical freedom of unions than employers.[8]

In addition, some academic observers have questioned whether the Board's rule making on substantive matters is necessary to attain the objectives of the NLRA. In suggesting and demonstrating that some of the regulatory rules are directed at behavior that has little or no impact on the objectives of the NLRA, these critics often propose at least partial deregulation of labor relations.[9] The analyses reported in this book assist in evaluating the merit of these alternative views and proposals.

6. AFL-CIO Committee on the Evolution of Work, *The Changing Situation of Workers and Their Unions* (Washington: AFL-CIO, 1985); Paul Weiler, "Promises to Keep: Securing Workers' Rights to Self-Organization under the NLRA" and "Striking a New Balance: Freedom of Contract and the Prospects for Union Representation," *Harvard Law Review,* vol. 96 (June 1983), pp. 1769–1827, and vol. 98 (December 1984), pp. 351–420; Richard B. Freeman and James L. Medoff, *What Do Unions Do?* (Basic Books, 1984).

7. James B. Atleson, *Values and Assumptions in American Labor Law* (University of Massachusetts Press, 1983); Paul A. Levy, ed., "The Unidimensional Perspective of the Reagan Labor Board," *Rutgers Law Journal,* vol. 16 (Winter 1985), pp. 269–390.

8. *Labor Law Reform Act of 1978,* Hearing before the Senate Committee on Human Resources, 95 Cong. 2 sess. (Government Printing Office, 1978); testimony of Richard L. Trumka, president of the United Mine Workers of America, in *Oversight Hearings on the Subject "Has Labor Law Failed,"* Joint Hearings before the Subcommittee on Labor-Management Relations of the House Committee on Education and Labor and the Manpower and Housing Subcommittee of the House Committee on Government Operations, 98 Cong. 2 sess. (GPO, 1984), pt. 1, pp. 3–27; interview with Lane Kirkland, president of the AFL-CIO, in Cathy Trost and Leonard M. Apcar, "AFL-CIO Chief Calls Labor Laws a 'Dead Letter,' " *Wall Street Journal,* August 16, 1984.

9. Derek C. Bok, "The Regulation of Campaign Tactics in Representation Elections Under the National Labor Relations Act," *Harvard Law Review,* vol. 78 (November 1964), pp. 38–141; Julius G. Getman, Stephen B. Goldberg, and Jeanne B. Herman, *Union Representation Elections: Law and Reality* (New York: Russell Sage Foundation, 1976); William T. Dickens, "The Effect of Company Campaigns on Certification Elections: *Law and Reality* Once Again," *Industrial and Labor Relations Review,* vol. 36 (July 1983), pp. 560–75.

Chapter 2 reviews the general features and implications of labor relations policy under the Nationʒl Labor Relations Act. Chapter 3 then develops the puzzle of the growing gap between the level of regulatory activity and the level of labor relations activities that are subject to regulation. It compares the outcome of U.S. policy with outcomes in Canada and Japan, which have a similar approach to labor relations policy. Chapter 4 evaluates the controversy regarding the effect of NLRB regulations on labor relations outcomes. Chapter 5 analyzes the influence of compliance and enforcement incentives on the growth of unfair labor practice charges.

This study finds that the litigation explosion in labor relations has occurred in virtually all categories of unfair labor practice and therefore cannot be traced to the effects of one or two key decisions on legal doctrine by the NLRB or the appellate courts. Moreover, shifts in the distribution of labor relations activity from regions and industries where resistance to unions is low to sectors where resistance is high explains only part of the growth of unfair labor practice charges (chapter 3).

Instead, much of the growth of regulatory litigation appears to be a general behavioral response to changing incentives to comply with and enforce compliance with the NLRA. Prominent among these is the growth of the difference between the cost of union labor and the cost of nonunion labor during the 1970s, which provided incentives to employers (who had more to lose) to violate the act and to unions (who had more to gain) to file charges challenging noncompliance with the act. The influence of the Board on compliance and enforcement incentives is muted, because it is not permitted to issue punitive remedies. Indeed, an important lesson of the analysis of the compliance process under the NLRA is that the volume of regulatory litigation is often driven by incentives that are beyond the influence of regulatory procedures. Regression analyses based on compliance incentives provide a better explanation of the growth of unfair labor practice charges than analyses based on the volume of labor relations activity and general economic conditions. Nevertheless, some of the growth of charges over time remains unexplained by any of these factors and may be associated with the gradual extension of rights under the law or shifts in the number of employers who approach the law strategically (chapter 5).

The study also finds that the effects of NLRA regulation on labor relations and unionization are often overstated. Earlier studies, although uneven, find that many of the rules developed by the NLRB may not be needed to establish the right to concerted activity provided by the act. Yet most studies find that delays in adjudication reduce the likelihood of a union victory in a representation election and otherwise interfere with this right. Even rules that are neutral in their effect on the right to concerted activity may produce an indirect interference by contributing to congestion and delay. Whatever the exact influence of noncompliance on collective bargaining rights, neither the overall volume of litigation nor litigation challenging suspected noncompliance by employers is a major source of the decline in unionization in the United States. This is so because unionization is the outcome of many factors, only some of which are influenced by regulation. During the 1970s, the increasing relative wage of union workers stimulated more profound adjustments in the use of union labor (chapter 4). Chapter 6 considers the implications of these findings for changes in national labor relations policy ranging from changes in remedies and procedures within the existing regulatory framework to repeal of the NLRA.

CHAPTER 2

Federal Policy toward Labor Relations

THE GROWTH of labor unions presents nations with significant questions of public policy. Should the government mandate collective bargaining? Should it otherwise assist in the process of establishing unions? What limits, if any, should be placed on the use of force, notably strikes and lockouts, in collective bargaining? Such questions are difficult to answer because efforts by workers to improve their working conditions with collective as well as individual actions in the labor market raise conflicts between the right to take concerted action and freedom of contract, between a system of private collective bargaining and the public interest in minimizing disruptions of commerce, and between majority rule and individual rights.

Different countries have answered these questions in different ways, but there appear to be two broad approaches to the formulation of labor relations policy. One is based on the principle of consensus, in which labor and management develop a set of general rules that is to govern their conduct in labor relations without government assistance. Procedural questions pertaining to how unions will come to be recognized as representatives of groups of workers, the conduct of collective bargaining, the termination of the collective bargaining agreement, and so on are determined by the parties to collective bargaining themselves. Scandinavian countries have taken this approach, often with the hope of forestalling direct government intervention in labor-management relations. Many observers believe that the parties to collective bargaining are more likely to bear responsibility for adhering to rules that they develop themselves than to rules imposed by third parties.

The other approach to labor relations, based on the principle of majority rule, has guided public policy in the United States. Rules

7

pertaining to the conduct of labor-management relations are established by legislation rather than by negotiation between the parties to collective bargaining. Under majority rule the preferences of minority interest groups receive little attention. If minority groups are sufficiently opposed to legislative requirements, they may try to circumvent the objectives of the policy by taking advantage of loopholes in the law. The frequent response to such efforts at evasion is more detailed rule making by legislative or administrative bodies. This in turn encourages a search for new loopholes and more rule making to close them. The result can be an extremely litigious regulatory system.

The National Labor Relations Act

With the passage of the National Labor Relations Act, the United States adopted the majority-rule approach to labor relations policy.[1] The NLRA now consists of the Wagner Act of 1935 (named for its chief sponsor) as amended by the Taft-Hartley Act of 1947 and certain provisions in the Landrum-Griffin Act of 1959. It regulates labor relations at the federal level.

Before passage of the Wagner Act, union growth had been slower in the United States than in other countries. By 1930, for example, 8.9 percent of the U.S. work force was unionized, while unions represented 36.0 percent of the work force in Sweden, 33.7 percent in Germany, and 25.7 percent in Great Britain.[2] It was generally believed that the main impediments to the more rapid spread of unions were the legal climate and the tactics of employer resistance.

Before the 1930s, labor unions and labor relations outside of the railroad industry were regulated according to the principles of common law, whose competitive orientation was often inimical to the interests of unions.[3] By the twentieth century the main legal impediments to union

1. Labor-management relations are also influenced by the Norris-LaGuardia Act of 1932, 47 Stat. 70, chap. 90 (1932), and, in the railroad and airline industries, by the Railway Labor Act of 1926, 44 Stat. 577, chap. 347 (1926). These statutes have much less influence on labor relations than the NLRA.

2. George Sayers Bain and Robert Price, *Profiles of Union Growth: A Comparative Statistical Portrait of Eight Countries* (Oxford: Basil Blackwell, 1980), p. 170.

3. Charles O. Gregory, *Labor and the Law*, 2d rev. ed. (Norton, 1961); Selig Perlman, *A History of Trade Unionism in the United States* (Macmillan, 1922), chap. 7; Richard A. Epstein, "A Common Law for Labor Relations: A Critique of the New

organizing were labor injunctions, which could be used to halt strikes in support of recognition or economic demands, and the enforcement of so-called yellow-dog contracts.[4] The Norris-LaGuardia Act of 1932 greatly circumscribed the use of injunctions in labor disputes and rendered yellow-dog contracts unenforceable in the federal courts.

Employers remained free to use other methods to resist unionization, however, and efforts to organize were frequently accompanied by strikes and violence as employers used espionage, detectives, strikebreakers, armed guards, and discharge of union supporters to thwart unions. Some employers adopted more sedate approaches, providing novel fringe benefits and sponsoring "company unions"—employee representation organizations financed and controlled by the company.

Against this background, Congress clearly intended to reverse the pro-competition tilt of common law by encouraging the growth of collective bargaining with the passage of the NLRA in 1935.[5] The conflict between the general statement of national policy in support of collective bargaining and the purported effects of the subsequent administration of the law have inspired strong criticism of the act and the NLRB.

To further its goal, Congress sought to reduce strike activity by prohibiting practices that encourage strikes over union recognition.[6] The act also expresses congressional concern that "inequality of bargaining

---

Deal Labor Legislation," *Yale Law Journal*, vol. 92 (July 1983), pp. 1357–1408; Richard A. Posner, "Some Economics of Labor Law," *University of Chicago Law Review*, vol. 51 (Fall 1984), pp. 988–1011.

4. The yellow-dog contract required employees to agree not to join a union as a condition of employment. Union organizers could therefore be held responsible for breach of contract.

5. Section 1 of the act states: "The denial by employers of the right of employees to organize and the refusal by employers to accept the procedure of collective bargaining lead to strikes and other forms of industrial strife or unrest, which have the intent or the necessary effect of burdening or obstructing commerce. . . . Experience has proved that protection by law of the right of employees to organize and bargain collectively safeguards commerce. . . . It is hereby declared to be the policy of the United States to . . . mitigate and eliminate these obstructions [to the free flow of commerce] . . . by encouraging the practice and procedure of collective bargaining and by protecting the exercise by workers of full freedom of association, self-organization, and designation of representatives of their own choosing, for the purpose of negotiating the terms and conditions of their employment or other mutual aid or protection." 49 Stat. 449–50 (1935).

6. The congressional intention was to remove "certain recognized sources of industrial strife" and to encourage "practices fundamental to the friendly adjustment of industrial disputes." 49 Stat. 449 (1935).

power . . . burdens . . . the flow of commerce and tends to aggravate recurrent business depressions, by depressing wage rates and . . . purchasing power.''[7] Concern for the economy is much less emphasized in regulatory decisions today than in 1935, however.

One way in which the National Labor Relations Act addressed labor problems was by granting all employees (not just union members) a broad right to engage in concerted activities in support of their interests as employees. This statutory right is the centerpiece of labor relations policy, for it appears to permit a broad range of collective activities by workers, going far beyond the traditional limits of negotiations between unions and management over the terms of a labor agreement.

The NLRA establishes an election procedure supervised by a government agency, the National Labor Relations Board, to determine which union, if any, will have the right to represent a group of employees. This aspect of the law provided the most direct contribution toward reducing strikes, for unions previously had had to strike to win their demands for recognition. Under the NLRA, a union winning the support of a majority of employees in a representation election becomes the exclusive bargaining representative of all employees in the bargaining unit. Exclusive representation, a status that is not generally accorded unions in European countries, places a legal obligation on the union to represent all workers in the unit, including those who may have voted against it in the representation election.[8] It also prevents employees from bargaining individually with the employer, thus increasing the security of unions by reducing the scope for challenges from nonsupporters. The legislation tends to stabilize labor relations by reducing the number of unions that an employer must deal with in a single bargaining unit.

The NLRA proscribes certain unfair labor practices. In the original Wagner Act, those proscriptions were intended to end some of the

7. Ibid. Some observers have argued that over the history of the NLRA the courts have given at least as much emphasis in their decisions to protecting management prerogatives from collective bargaining and to preserving the mobility of capital. James B. Atleson, *Values and Assumptions in American Labor Law* (University of Massachusetts Press, 1983), p. 135, argues: ''Although the law creates protections for unions, it makes no attempt to equalize bargaining power, and indeed the court has slapped down the Board when it attempted to consider relative bargaining power in reaching a decision.''

8. In 1947 the Taft-Hartley Act introduced decertification elections (also supervised by the NLRB) in which workers vote on whether to remove an exclusive bargaining representative; it assigned to the NLRB the responsibility of investigating and adjudicating charges of unfair labor practices.

employer tactics that had been seen as impediments to self-organization by workers. The act prohibits employers from interfering with efforts by employees to exercise their rights to concerted activity, from dominating or assisting employee organizations financially or in any other way, from discriminating on the basis of union activity in their treatment of individuals, from punishing individuals who give testimony in legal proceedings related to the enforcement of the act, and from bargaining in bad faith.[9]

The Taft-Hartley amendments established a list of unfair practices on the part of unions and sharpened the language applied to employer practices. It prohibits unions from interfering with employees' exercise of their right to join or refrain from concerted activity, from forcing an employer to discriminate against an employee for reasons other than nonpayment of union dues, from refusing to bargain, from engaging in secondary boycotts, from forcing an employer to pay for services that are not performed, and from certain other practices.[10]

9. Section 8.a of the NLRA states: "It shall be an unfair labor practice for an employer—(1) to interfere with, restrain, or coerce employees in the exercise of the rights guaranteed in section 7; (2) to dominate or interfere with the formation or administration of any labor organization or contribute financial or other support to it . . . ; (3) by discrimination in regard to hire or tenure of employment or any term or condition of employment to encourage or discourage membership in any labor organization . . . ; (4) to discharge or otherwise discriminate against an employee because he has filed charges or given testimony under this Act; (5) to refuse to bargain collectively with the representatives of his employees, subject to the provisions of section 9 (a)." 49 Stat. 452–53 (1935), as amended, 61 Stat. 140–41 (1947).

10. Section 8.b of the NLRA states: "It shall be an unfair labor practice for a labor organization or its agents—(1) to restrain or coerce (A) employees in the exercise of the rights guaranteed [in this Act] . . . ; or (B) an employer in the selection of his representatives for the purpose of collective bargaining or the adjustment of grievances; (2) to cause or attempt to cause an employer to discriminate against an employee in violation of subsection (a) (3) or to discriminate against an employee with respect to whom membership in such organization has been denied or terminated on some ground other than his failure to tender the periodic dues and the initiation fees uniformly required as a condition of acquiring or retaining membership; (3) to refuse to bargain collectively with an employer . . . ; (4) [to engage in secondary boycotts]; (5) to require of employees covered by an agreement authorized under subsection (a) (3) the payment, as a condition precedent to becoming a member of such organization, of a fee in an amount which the Board finds excessive or discriminatory under all the circumstances . . . ; (6) to cause or attempt to cause an employer to pay or deliver or agree to pay or deliver any money or other thing of value, in the nature of an exaction, for services which are not performed or not to be performed; and (7) [to engage in organizational picketing to pressure an employer to recognize a union without a representation election]." 61 Stat. 141–42 (1947), as amended, 73 Stat. 544 (1959).

Administration of the Act by the NLRB

The NLRA provides a legal framework for managing two aspects of the relationship between employers and workers—the establishment of unions, and the formation and implementation of the employment agreement—as well as aspects of the relationship between unions and their members. However, the specific rules governing these relations are developed through the day-to-day decisions of the NLRB.[11] In reaching its decisions, the Board has attempted to determine whether the specific complaints of illegal behavior emanating from the daily conduct of labor relations fall into one of the statutory concepts of an unfair labor practice. Its decisions, over fifty years, have created an elaborate set of rules and doctrines governing union and management conduct in labor relations that contrasts sharply with the broad statutory definitions of unfair labor practices.

Formation of Unions

A union-organizing drive usually begins with a union soliciting employee signatures on cards that authorize the union to represent the employee in collective bargaining with the employer. If a majority of workers in the proposed bargaining unit sign authorization cards, the employer may recognize the union without the formality of an election, but this rarely occurs. Instead, the union presents a petition for a representation election to the NLRB, which requires authorization cards signed by at least 30 percent of the employees before it will order an election.

Once the NLRB accepts a petition to hold an election, it has considerable authority over the process of union formation. Initially, the Board determines the scope of the election unit—which group of employees will be eligible to vote in the election—either by accepting a joint proposal from the union and the employer involved in the election or, in the minority of cases where the two sides cannot agree, by making its own unit determination after hearing the arguments on each side. This determination may influence the outcome of the election, the scope of the future bargaining unit (assuming that the employees vote for repre-

11. The Board is composed of five members appointed for staggered five-year terms. No more than three members may be affiliated with the same political party.

sentation), and the relative bargaining power of the parties. After a campaign in which union and employer attempt to persuade employees in the unit to accept or reject union representation, the Board conducts a secret-ballot election. If the union wins, the Board certifies it as the exclusive bargaining representative of the workers in the unit. The Board also investigates and adjudicates any allegations of unfair labor practice growing out of the campaign preceding the election.[12]

In its regulation of the union organizing process, the Board must balance the right of workers to self-organization, which is guaranteed by section 7 of the NLRA, with the First Amendment guarantee of freedom of expression to all parties, including employers, which is codified in section 8.c. In evaluating allegations of illegal campaign behavior, the NLRB seeks "to provide a laboratory in which an experiment may be conducted, under conditions as nearly ideal as possible, to determine the uninhibited desires of the employees."[13] Many observers doubt that this standard (which is not required by the statute) is attainable, given the uncertainty about what determines voting behavior.[14] The Board has developed an extensive set of rules on the access of union organizers to employees; the form, content, and accuracy of campaign speeches by union and management; and acts of discrimination by employers against union supporters. It may sustain an objection to conduct during the election campaign that falls short of committing an unfair labor practice and rerun the election. It may also set aside the election's results if it finds merit in an unfair practice charge filed by the losing party. And, if an employer's unfair labor practices are believed to preclude the possibility of an untainted new election, the Board may certify a union that has lost an election as the workers' bargaining representative if a majority of the employees in the unit had signed authorization cards.[15]

12. The same basic procedures apply to decertification elections, but the process is initiated by a petition claiming that a majority of the employees in the bargaining unit do not wish to be represented by the current bargaining agent.

13. *General Shoe Corp.*, 77 N.L.R.B. 124, 127 (1948).

14. Derek C. Bok, "The Regulation of Campaign Tactics in Representation Elections Under the National Labor Relations Act," *Harvard Law Review*, vol. 78 (November 1964), pp. 38–141.

15. *NLRB* v. *Gissel Packing Co.*, 395 U.S. 575 (1969). Some U.S. courts of appeals have accepted (in cases of severe and pervasive unfair labor practices) the propriety of bargaining orders when only a minority of employees initially signed authorization cards. For a brief period the Board included "nonmajority" bargaining orders in its remedies but then reverted to the majority requirement. See *Conair Corp.*, 261 N.L.R.B. 1189 (1982); *Gourmet Foods, Inc.*, 270 N.L.R.B. 578 (1984).

Almost 30 percent of the unfair labor practice charges filed with the NLRB are associated with efforts to form unions.[16] The Board has conducted 8,000 to 9,000 elections annually since the mid-1960s. Between 1950 and 1981 the proportion of elections won by unions declined from 74.5 percent to 45.4 percent. While the number of decertification elections increased from 112 to 856, the union success rate in these elections declined from 33.0 percent in 1950 to 25.1 percent in 1981.[17]

The regulation of union election campaigns has become a major source of contention between labor and management. As union membership declines, unions tend to blame their losses on the rise of unfair labor practices by employers and the use of management consultants specializing in union avoidance tactics that include operating on the fringe of NLRB doctrine. (The mixed evidence on this proposition is discussed in chapter 4.)

Conduct of Collective Bargaining

The role of the National Labor Relations Board does not end with the representation election. Indeed, an estimated 30 percent of all charges of unfair labor practice pertain to the collective bargaining process.[18] But because Congress wished to maintain a private system of collective bargaining, the National Labor Relations Act gives the NLRB no authority to impose contractual terms or to render judgments (as do arbitrators in certain circumstances) concerning what a fair outcome to a collective bargaining dispute would be. Nor does the NLRB have authority to mediate labor disputes.[19] But to ensure that workers who elect a union representative will receive some of the benefits of a collective bargaining relationship, the NLRA does impose a duty on both parties to bargain in good faith.

Over the past fifty years, the implementation of the duty to bargain has resulted in the development of rules governing both the conduct and the substance of collective bargaining. The Board forbids conduct (refusal to meet or furnish information, stalling tactics, and the like) that

16. Estimate derived from a random sample of unfair labor practices closed in fiscal 1976 by Myron J. Roomkin and Dawn A. Harris in "Interindustry Patterns in Unfair Labor Practice Cases," *Journal of Labor Research*, vol. 5 (Spring 1984), pp. 113–26.

17. *Annual Report of the National Labor Relations Board*, various years, statistical appendix.

18. Roomkin and Harris, "Interindustry Patterns," p. 125.

19. The Federal Mediation and Conciliation Service has this authority.

it finds an obstacle to a full exchange of views. It has also been drawn into developing regulations on substantive issues because the NLRA requirement that the parties bargain over "wages, hours, and other terms and conditions of employment" is open ended. In its effort to distinguish between legal and illegal refusals to bargain over a "term or condition of employment" in dispute, the Board has developed a three-way classification of issues. Issues that involve a violation of some law are termed illegal and therefore need not be bargained; issues that the Board finds within the meaning of "other terms and conditions of employment" are termed mandatory, and issues that do not fall within the first two meanings are termed voluntary. Refusal to bargain over voluntary or illegal issues is not judged an unfair labor practice, even if the refusal causes a work stoppage. Bargaining over a voluntary issue to the point of impasse, however, has been ruled an unfair practice, on the grounds that the NLRA does not condone work stoppages over issues that are peripheral to labor relations.[20]

As new issues are introduced into bargaining, the parties often do not know what is mandatory and what is voluntary until one side refuses to bargain and an unfair labor practice charge is filed and adjudicated. Increases in the number of issues introduced into collective bargaining can therefore increase the number of issues that turn out to constitute unfair practices. The classification scheme can also alter the relative bargaining power of labor and management on any given issue. By defining which demands can be backed by strikes or lockouts (the mandatory issues) and which cannot (the voluntary issues), the Board may have an influence on the choice of issues that end up in the employment contract and therefore on the substantive outcome of collective bargaining, contrary to the intention of Congress.

The practical effect of the duty to bargain on the attainment of collective bargaining agreements is also uncertain. Neither party is under any legal obligation to make concessions or reach any agreement, let alone one that leaves members of the bargaining unit in a better position than they would have been without a union.[21] The fact that in recent years about a third of the unions winning representation elections have not succeeded in negotiating a labor agreement suggests some ineffectiveness in the provision.[22] More than any other area of the administration

20. *NLRB* v. *Wooster Division of Borg-Warner Corp.*, 356 U.S. 342, 349 (1958).
21. *White* v. *NLRB*, 255 F. 2d 564 (5th Cir. 1958).
22. Richard Prosten, "The Longest Season: Union Organizing in the Last Decade,

of the NLRA, the duty to bargain has been condemned by academic observers as an intrusion into the bargaining process and a requirement that has no practical value in labor relations.[23]

In the face of employer opposition, the existence and content of a collective bargaining agreement will be determined by the relative bargaining power of labor and management. Under current law, the only way for a union to respond to an employer who fulfills the bargaining requirement but avoids signing an agreement is to use economic coercion—a strike—in support of its demands. The success of the tactic again depends on bargaining power—this time the amount of effective coercion generated by a strike. But this is exactly the alternative that would be available to unions in the absence of a duty to bargain. The legal duty may get parties to sit at the same table, but the force that ultimately drives them to an agreement is the configuration of their relative bargaining power.

Economic Coercion

Work stoppages and the ability to compel agreement by the threat of a stoppage are at the heart of the collective bargaining process. Workers in the United States do not have a constitutional right to strike. That right must be provided by statute, as it is for workers in the private sector by the Norris-LaGuardia Act and particularly by the seemingly broad protection to concerted activities by employees granted in section 7 of the NLRA. The protections are not as broad as it might appear, however.

The key to a statutory right to strike is the reinstatement right accorded to striking employees. Technically, the legal right to strike only prohibits employers from discharging or disciplining employees who engage in peaceful strikes, and the Supreme Court ruled long ago that an employer has a right to hire permanent replacements for employees engaged in a normal economic strike. Employees' reinstatement rights after a strike only give them preference for employment as vacancies occur. The

a/k/a How Come One Team Has to Play with Its Shoelaces Tied Together?'' in Barbara D. Dennis, ed., *Proceedings of the Thirty-First Annual Meeting of the Industrial Relations Research Association* (Madison, Wisc.: IRRA, 1979), p. 247.

23. Archibald Cox, "The Duty to Bargain in Good Faith," *Harvard Law Review*, vol. 71 (June 1958), pp. 1401–42; R. W. Fleming, "The Obligation to Bargain in Good Faith," *Virginia Law Review*, vol. 47 (October 1961), pp. 988–1013.

employer is not obliged to fire workers hired during the strike to provide jobs for returning strikers.[24] On the other hand, striking workers have an absolute right to reinstatement when a strike is the result of unfair labor practices by the employer. Thus, there is an obvious incentive for unions to file charges of unfair practice during strikes in which it appears that the employer may be inclined to hire replacements.

Employers also have a right to lock out workers when a labor agreement has expired and bargaining has reached an impasse.[25] Workers who are locked out have an absolute right of replacement, however.

The NLRA also limits employees' right to strike in other ways. Wildcat strikes—stoppages in violation of a contractual no-strike clause—are illegal, as are violent strikes and work stoppages aimed at inducing an employer to violate the law.[26] In addition, secondary boycotts by unions against neutral employers are forbidden. There is an interesting and frequently criticized asymmetry in the enforcement of the law in this area. In most cases, there is no attempt to rectify an alleged unfair labor practice until after the charge is adjudicated. In the case of allegations of secondary boycotts and certain forms of illegal picketing by unions, however, the regional offices of the NLRB are required to seek an immediate injunction to halt the alleged violation until after the charge has been adjudicated.

Rights of Individual Employees

Over the years, the NLRB has broadened the concept of concerted activity protected by section 7 of the NLRA. In the mid-1960s, it ruled that the assertion by a single worker of rights common to other workers under an existing collective bargaining agreement constituted concerted activity protected by the NLRA.[27] And subsequently the Board held that action by any employee, whether unionized or not, in support of

24. *NLRB* v. *Mackay Radio and Telegraph Co.*, 304 U.S. 333 (1938). Strikers who have been replaced also retain for one year their right to vote in any NLRB elections that might occur to determine the union's status in the plant.

25. *American Ship Building Co.* v. *NLRB*, 380 U.S. 300 (1965).

26. Strikes that threaten to cause substantial economic hardship or present significant health or safety problems to the general public are not forbidden, but the Taft-Hartley Act provides for "emergency dispute procedures" that may be initiated by the president to try to find a solution to the dispute short of a strike. 61 Stat. 155–56 (1947).

27. *Interboro Contractors, Inc.*, 157 N.L.R.B. 1295 (1966). This interpretation of the act was later upheld by the Supreme Court in *NLRB* v. *City Disposal Systems, Inc.*, 465 U.S. 822 (1984).

rights guaranteed to all workers under a state or federal law was protected concerted activity.[28] Although the NLRB in 1984 reversed the doctrine protecting individually asserted rights that were common to all employees,[29] its expansive interpretation of concerted activity during the 1960s and 1970s may have contributed to the general increase in regulatory activity.

Similarly, the Supreme Court agreed with the Board in 1975 that an employer who refused to permit a union representative (and later, any other employee) to be present during a disciplinary interview of an employee was guilty of an unlawful refusal to bargain.[30] Moreover, the Court held that an employee cannot be discharged for exercising this right. This too expanded the redress to individual workers provided by the NLRA.

Enforcement Procedures

When one of the parties to collective bargaining files an unfair labor practice charge, the NLRB first conducts an audit of the alleged misbehavior. For the party filing charges, the cost of initiating an audit is low, since the Board (or the federal courts in an appeal) bears most of the cost of investigating the merits of the charge. By the late 1970s, over 40,000 audits per year were being initiated by unions, employers, and workers.

It is unusual to assign a single agency the responsibility of both prosecuting and adjudicating alleged violations of the law. In order to avoid a conflict of interest, an Office of General Counsel in the NLRB handles the agency's administrative activities, conducting representation elections and investigating and prosecuting charges of unfair labor practice, and the Board itself adjudicates cases that reach it. The regional offices of the NLRB make the initial investigation of unfair practice charges and the vast majority are dismissed or withdrawn at that stage (during the 1970s, approximately one-third were dismissed, another third withdrawn). When the regional office finds that a charge has merit, a complaint is issued and a hearing by one of the Board's administrative law judges is scheduled at the regional level. (In a typical year, 20–25

28. *Alleluia Cushions, Co.*, 221 N.L.R.B. 999 (1975).
29. *Meyers Industries, Inc.*, 268 N.L.R.B. 493 (1984).
30. *NLRB* v. *Weingarten, Inc.*, 420 U.S. 251 (1975).

percent of the charges filed—or 6–8 percent of the cases judged to have merit—are settled before a decision is issued by an administrative law judge.) The General Counsel's Office typically argues the plaintiff's case in this hearing. The administrative law judge issues a decision, which is usually appealed to the Board in Washington, D.C. In recent years about 5 percent of the unfair labor practice charges (2 percent of the charges having merit) that are filed eventually reach the Board. The case is then considered by either a panel of three Board members or, in particularly important cases, the entire Board.[31]

If a majority of the Board members determines that an unfair labor practice has occurred, the Board issues an order that the offending party "cease and desist" from the behavior that gave rise to the charge; it may also order some form of remedial action. The Board has no authority to enforce its cease-and-desist order, however; it must seek enforcement by the United States Court of Appeals. The appeals court generally accepts the facts developed by the NLRB and reviews the case to determine whether the law has been applied properly. In about 75 percent of the cases, the Board's position is sustained in whole or in part. Either party can appeal a decision of the appeals court to the U.S. Supreme Court, where many of the most far-reaching decisions concerning the regulation of labor relations have been made.

The entire process of resolving unfair labor practice charges has become increasingly time consuming, and congressional oversight and appropriations committees have frequently voiced concern over the Board's backload of cases. Virtually all of the delay within the Board has occurred at the adjudication stage. The time taken for the initial screening of cases by the regional offices of the NLRB—the process that results in the withdrawal or dismissal of most of the charges—has declined slightly since the early 1960s. Since the early 1970s, however, the average time between the issuance of a complaint and a decision by an administrative law judge has increased from four months to nine and a half months (table 2-1). For Board decisions that are appealed, there is a further delay, which has increased from an average of about one year in the early 1970s to about sixteen months in the early 1980s. These delays play an important part in determining the extent to which the objectives of the NLRA are obtained in the administration of the statute.

31. Disposition of charges is reported in the statistical appendix to the *Annual Report of the NLRB*.

Table 2-1. **Average Median Days Elapsed in Processing Unfair Labor Practice Cases, 1963–65, 1973–75, and 1980–82**

Process	1963–65	1973–75	1980–82
Filing of charge to Board's decision	354	338	468
Filing to complaint	55	52	45
Complaint to close of hearing before administrative law judge	58	54	153
Close of hearing to judge's decision	95	72	141
Judge's decision to Board's decision	122	133	124
Board's decision to court of appeals' decision	n.a.	362	483

Source: *Departments of Labor, Health and Human Services, Education, and Related Agencies Appropriations for 1985,* Hearings before the Subcommittee on the Departments of Labor, Health and Human Services, Education, and Related Agencies of the House Committee on Appropriations, 98 Cong. 2 sess. (Government Printing Office, 1984), pt. 7: *Related Agencies,* p. 641.
n.a. Not available.

The growing litigiousness associated with labor relations policy also imposes costs on the federal court system. In 1961, the 425 NLRB cases taken to the U.S. courts of appeals represented 10 percent of the courts' caseload (the postwar peak). Since then, the number of cases appealed or brought for enforcement of Board orders has more than doubled, averaging 911 in 1980–83, but the total caseload of the appeals courts has increased so much more rapidly that NLRB cases accounted for 3.4 percent of the courts' cases.[32] Over the past two decades, the number of NLRB cases going to the U.S. Supreme Court has remained at about five per year, constituting 2–3 percent of the Court's workload.[33]

Remedial Action

A central policy issue of recent decades has been the limits placed on the corrective actions that the National Labor Relations Board may construct. The Supreme Court has ruled that Board actions must be remedial rather than punitive, and that the objective should be to restore the status quo in labor relations that existed at the time of a violation. Thus when employers are found at fault, the Board usually requires them to post cease-and-desist orders that all employees may see (about 5,000 notices per year were posted in the late 1970s). When workers have been illegally discharged, the Board typically orders their reinstatement with

32. *Annual Report of the Director of the Administrative Office of the United States Courts,* various issues.
33. "The Supreme Court, 1960 Term," *Harvard Law Review,* vol. 75 (November 1961), table 2, and subsequent November issues.

back pay. For an employer's refusal to bargain, it may issue an order to bargain. Where it finds evidence of a company union, it will order the disestablishment of the union. And when it finds illegal picketing or work stoppages by unions, the NLRB will order an end to the unlawful activity.

Current remedies are unlikely to restore the status quo in labor relations. For example, the number of NLRB orders for reinstatement of illegally discharged union supporters rose from 922 in 1957 (the postwar low) to 3,779 in 1970 to 10,033 in 1980. Awards for back pay in those years mounted from $601,059 to $3,749,370 to $32,135,914.[34] Given the months and sometimes years consumed in investigating and adjudicating the allegations of illegal discharge, however, most workers had found other jobs or moved by the time an order for their reinstatement was issued. Others feared further mistreatment by the company. As a result only a minority accepted reinstatement, with the percentage decreasing as the time taken to adjudicate the charge increased.[35] The net result was hardly the maintenance of the status quo in labor relations. Instead, the effect of letting a contested action (a discharge) stand until final adjudication was to push union support below its original levels.

Orders to bargain seem equally unsuccessful. Collective bargaining was initiated as the result of NLRB remedial orders in over 2,000 cases a year in the late 1970s. These orders are issued either because an employer's refusal to bargain has been found illegal or because the employer's unfair labor practices are assumed to be so serious as to interfere with the free choice of employees during a union election campaign. In both instances, the outcome will ultimately depend more on the relative bargaining power of the parties than on the legal remedy. In fact, only 35–40 percent of the unions that obtain bargaining orders because of the interference with free choice ultimately succeed in negotiating a collective bargaining agreement.[36]

In view of the difficulty of restoring the status quo ante, the introduc-

34. Data provided by NLRB, Office of Statistical Services.

35. About 40 percent of those offered reinstatement in one region in the early 1970s accepted the remedy, with the rate dropping to 5 percent for workers who had been discharged more than six months earlier. Almost two-thirds of those accepting the remedy left the company within six months after reinstatement. Elvis C. Stephens and Warren Chaney, "A Study of the Reinstatement Remedy Under the National Labor Relations Act," *Labor Law Journal*, vol. 25 (January 1974), pp. 31–41.

36. Charles B. Craver, "The Current and Future Status of Labor Organizations," in Labor Law Group, *The Park City Papers* (Nashville: The Group, 1985), p. 76.

Table 2-2. Budget Authority of Major Federal Regulatory Agencies, 1970 and 1983
Thousands of dollars

	Budget outlays	
Agency	*1970*	*1983*
National Labor Relations Board	37,703	122,639
Securities and Exchange Commission	21,513	89,905
Federal Communications Commission	23,639	81,628
Interstate Commerce Commission	27,464	61,577
Civil Aeronautics Board	11,184	23,640

Source: *Budget of the United States Government, Fiscal Year 1972* and *Fiscal Year 1985.*

tion of punitive damages for violations has often been urged. Indeed, one of the major objectives of the unsuccessful labor law reform legislation of 1977 was to provide stronger penalties for unfair labor practice violations. The potential role for punitive damages under the NLRA is analyzed in chapters 5 and 6.

Costs of the Regulatory Approach

The costs of regulating labor-management relations that appear in the federal budget indicate that the public resources required to support the activities of the NLRB are large in comparison to those of other long-established regulatory agencies (table 2-2). Public resources allocated to the regulation of labor relations policy far exceeded the government resources commanded by the Securities and Exchange Commission, the Federal Communications Commission, the Civil Aeronautics Board, and the Interstate Commerce Commission even before the deregulation of the last two agencies in the late 1970s.

Distribution of the NLRB budget by the Board's major activities shows that 70 percent is consumed by the field work of conducting union representation elections and investigating charges of unfair labor practices. About 18 percent goes to the adjudication activities of administrative law judges and the Board and the remaining 12 percent to enforcement activities.[37] There has been little change in these functional allocations over the postwar period.

As with other regulatory policies, the resource costs of the national labor relations policy are only partially revealed by federal budget data.

37. *Budget of the United States Government, Fiscal Year 1983—Appendix*, p. I–V113, and earlier issues.

Many of the costs of the regulatory requirements and compliance activities are borne by the parties regulated. It seems likely that the greatest part of these costs is the legal expenses the parties (usually employers) incur defending themselves against charges that they have violated the NLRA.

Regulation of the Labor Relations Process

Since few American employers appear to desire unionization, conflicts inevitably arise between unions and management over the methods used to persuade workers to join a union. The potential for conflict continues in the negotiation of collective bargaining agreements, perhaps more so during efforts to negotiate an initial agreement than in mature collective bargaining relationships. But the proposal of new topics in later bargaining talks may lead to duty-to-bargain charges. And when a strike is likely, unions may file charges of unfair labor practices in an effort to protect the reinstatement rights of their members. Also, conflicts between members and their unions over the administration of a collective bargaining agreement may give rise to charges alleging violations of the duty of fair representation.

There is no reason why the particular regulatory framework adopted in the United States need result in an explosion of regulatory activity. Yet the increasingly detailed rule making by the NLRB has not been accompanied by a reduction in regulatory activity. To the contrary, unfair practice charges have doubled in number every decade since the mid-1950s. The way in which this increase reflects changes in the relations between labor and management and in their incentives to comply with NLRB rulings is explored in the following chapters.

CHAPTER 3

The Growth of Regulatory Litigation

WHEN Congress passed the National Labor Relations Act in 1935, there was some expectation that labor and management would come to an implicit understanding on the "rules of the game" in labor relations and that the regulatory apparatus set up in the act would seldom be needed. Fifty years later, the most striking feature of U.S. labor relations policy is the sheer volume of regulatory activity. The number of unfair labor practice charges filed with the National Labor Relations Board (NLRB) was 6,807 in 1938, the year after the Supreme Court upheld the act's constitutionality,[1] and in the postwar period the number rose from 5,809 in 1950 to 44,063 in 1980.

What accounts for the remarkable growth of regulatory litigation? In principle, the growth of unfair labor practice charges could reflect expansions in the jurisdiction of the NLRA, changes in legal doctrine that alter the rights that are protected under the act, the response of the parties to labor relations to incentives for strategic behavior that are inherent in the regulatory framework itself, or some combination of these factors. In fact, little is known about how these factors affect the growth of litigation under the NLRA.

Accelerated Growth of Unfair Labor Practice Charges

For about ten years after the passage of the Taft-Hartley Act in 1947, when the NLRA was expanded to include unfair labor practices by unions as well as employers, the annual number of complaints filed with the National Labor Relations Board remained relatively stable. Since

1. *NLRB* v. *Jones and Laughlin Steel Corp.*, 301 U.S. 1 (1937).

24

the late 1950s, however, the annual number of new charges of unfair practices has doubled every decade. What caused the stark change in regulatory litigation under the NLRA that occurred around 1958?

Figure 3-1 shows how the patterns of charges by unions, employers, and individual workers vary. Charges by individual workers, which are often overlooked, have become an increasingly important aspect of regulatory litigation. Charges filed by workers against both employers and unions increased sharply over 1957-59, but then leveled off until the late 1960s. But growth in workers' charges is not the sole explanation for the growth in litigation in the late 1950s, for charges by unions and by employers also increased at that time, although less dramatically. In the late 1960s and throughout the 1970s charges by workers accelerated again and constituted an important element in the general growth of litigation under the NLRA. This second acceleration corresponds roughly with Supreme Court decisions expanding the concepts of fair representation and, later, of protected concerted activity, but it is by no means clear that these changes in legal doctrine are the main reasons for the increase in charges by individual workers.[2]

Charges by workers against unions and against employers are very tightly correlated (correlation coefficient of .992), which may reflect a tendency for workers to file charges simultaneously against the employers and unions involved in fair representation proceedings. The annual number of charges filed by workers is also closely and positively correlated with the number of charges filed by unions and by employers, which is contrary to the notion that workers would act primarily to compensate for the failure of unions or employers to challenge violations of labor relations law.[3]

A second feature of regulation under the NLRA is the preponderance of charges challenging employer behavior. In a typical year since 1948, about 70 percent of the charges filed were allegations of employer violations of the act, and those charges grew at a more rapid rate than

2. *Vaca* v. *Sipes,* 386 U.S. 171 (1967); *NLRB* v. *J. Weingarten, Inc.,* 420 U.S. 251 (1975). The Supreme Court's decision in *NLRB* v. *Gissel Packing Co.,* 395 U.S. 575 (1969), provided incentives for either unions or workers to file unfair labor practice charges during a representation campaign in order to build a case for a bargaining order if the election were lost, but it is not clear why workers rather than unions would be more likely to file.

3. The compensatory hypothesis implies a negative correlation between charges filed by workers and by unions or employers. In fact, the sample correlation coefficients for data displayed in fig. 3-1 are positive and lie between .89 and .98.

Figure 3-1. Charges of Unfair Labor Practices Filed with the NLRB, 1948–80

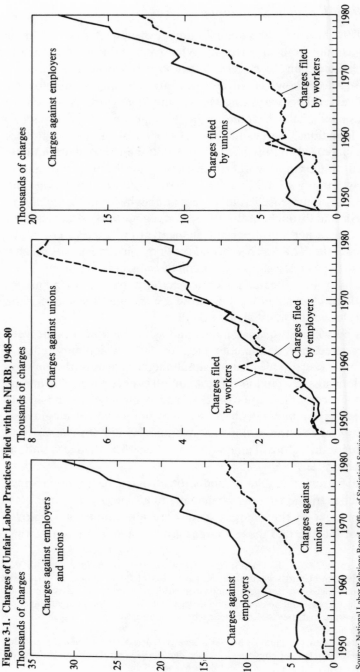

Source: National Labor Relations Board, Office of Statistical Services.

charges against unions after 1960. Indeed, during most of the 1970s there was little increase in the use of the regulatory system by employers to challenge union activities. Most of the growth in charges against unions during the 1970s came from workers, and between 1970 and 1980 the number of charges filed against unions by workers exceeded the number filed by employers. By 1980, 61 percent of the charges against unions and 42 percent of the charges against employers were filed by workers. Many observers attribute the difference in growth of charges filed by unions and by employers in the 1970s to a more thorough protection of the rights of management than of workers,[4] which may account for recent expressions of support for deregulation of labor relations by labor representatives and opposition to deregulation by management groups.[5]

A third feature of the regulation of labor relations in the United States is the across-the-board growth in litigation. The trends described in figure 3-1 cannot be traced to one or two key rulings by the NLRB or the courts, nor do they reflect litigation pertaining to one or two particular categories of unfair labor practice. Instead, allegations of labor law violations since 1948 have increased in every category of unfair labor practice established in the National Labor Relations Act (table 3-1). Charges against unions grew most rapidly in the decade following passage of the Taft-Hartley Act, and then declined in the 1960s and 1970s.[6] On the other hand, the growth of charges filed against employers for interference with the collective bargaining rights of their employees (section 8.a.1) has accelerated in each postwar decade. The main acceleration in the growth of charges alleging employer failures to bargain in good faith (section 8.a.5) occurred in the 1960s (over the 1950s). A

4. For example, see the testimony of Dan Pollitt, in *Oversight Hearings on the Subject "Has Labor Law Failed,"* Joint Hearings before the Subcommittee on Labor-Management Relations of the House Committee on Education and Labor and the Manpower and Housing Subcommittee of the House Committee on Government Operations, 98 Cong. 2 sess. (Government Printing Office, 1984), pt. 1, pp. 28–32.

5. Testimony of Richard L. Trumka, in ibid.; interview with Lane Kirkland, in Cathy Trost and Leonard M. Apcar, "AFL-CIO Chief Calls Labor Laws a 'Dead Letter,' " *Wall Street Journal,* August 16, 1984. The position of management in 1980 is quite different from the early stance; see James A. Gross, *The Making of the National Labor Relations Board: A Study in Economics, Politics, and the Law,* vol. 1: *1933–1937* (Albany: SUNY Press, 1974), p. 138; Irving Bernstein, *The New Deal Collective Bargaining Policy* (University of California Press, 1950), p. 100. Some of the change in position undoubtedly results from the restrictions placed on unions in the Taft-Hartley amendments to the act.

6. The results for charges filed under sections 8.b.5 and 6 can be discounted since the total in these categories is minute.

Table 3-1. Estimated Annual Growth in Charges of Unfair Labor Practices Filed, Various Periods, 1948–80

Percent

Charges filed under NLRA[a]	1948–80[b]	1948–60[b]	1961–70[b]	1971–80[b]
Against employers and unions	7.6	7.2	5.2	7.0
Against employers	7.1	5.4	9.9	8.0
Section 8.a.1	9.0	3.7[c]	6.9	15.0
Section 8.a.2	3.0	5.3[d]	−0.3	4.2
Section 8.a.3	6.6	6.5	3.3	7.0
Section 8.a.4	9.5	8.7	4.7	14.3
Section 8.a.5	7.9	1.6[e]	9.5	7.2
Against unions	8.7	12.1	6.4	4.8
Section 8.b.1	9.0	13.8	6.9	6.9
Section 8.b.2	3.4	12.7	−1.1[e]	−0.8[e]
Section 8.b.3	7.5	4.5[d]	10.0	4.9
Section 8.b.4	8.2	9.8	6.7	0.9[e]
Section 8.b.5	3.3	2.9[e]	5.9[c]	8.7
Section 8.b.6	1.7[d]	−8.6[d]	6.2[d]	12.5

Source: National Labor Relations Board, Office of Statistical Services.
a. For definitions of the NLRA subsections, see notes 9 and 10 in chap. 2.
b. The growth rate is estimated from the regression:

$$\ln ULP_{jt} = b_o + b_l \, TIME_t + e_{jt},$$

in which ln denotes the natural logarithm, ULP represents the number of unfair labor practice charges, j the section of the NLRA, t the year, $TIME$ the time trend, e the error, and b the rate of growth. Estimated rates of growth, b, are significant at the 1 percent level of confidence except where noted otherwise.
c. Significant at the 10 percent level.
d. Significant at the 5 percent level.
e. Not significant at conventional levels.

substantial acceleration in charges of general employer discrimination against union supporters (section 8.a.3) occurred in the 1970s.

During the 1970s there were also increases in most of the categories of remedial action taken by the NLRB (table 3-2). Increases in remedies for discriminatory discharge appeared to be particularly dramatic toward the end of the decade. But there was no noticeable trend in the real value of back pay awarded. Only in the small number of instances in which union recognition was withdrawn, an employer-dominated union was disestablished, or a work stoppage was ended did the Board's remedial actions decline over the decade.

The broad facts about growth of regulatory litigation under the NLRA reveal how varied the causes are. The dominance of charges against employers suggests that management may be a little restrained by the act. But with charges filed by workers against unions increasing, the growth of litigation cannot be interpreted as solely a symptom of employer efforts to thwart unions. While workers may sometimes serve

**Table 3-2. Remedial Actions Taken in Unfair Labor Practice Cases,
Various Years, 1948–80**

Action	1948	1960	1965	1970	1975	1980
			Number of cases			
Against employers						
Notice posted	384	2,299	2,688	3,003	3,970	4,894
Employees offered reinstatement	n.a.	n.a.	1,122	952	1,532	2,851
Back pay distributed	n.a.	n.a.	1,467	1,660	2,249	3,984
Collective bargaining begun	196	315	1,175	1,657	1,624	2,227
Work stoppage ended	n.a.	n.a.	184	349	199	198
Employer-dominated union disestablished	37	33	37	37	33	10
			Number of workers			
In favor of workers						
Reinstatement offered	1,001	1,885	5,875	3,779	3,816	10,033
Back wages paid	1,196	2,923	4,591	6,806	7,393	15,566
			Thousands of 1948 dollars			
Total back pay awarded	431	926	2,123	2,324	5,048	9,388

Source: NLRB, Office of Statistical Services.
n.a. Not available.

as a surrogate for their union in filing charges for tactical reasons, the increase in charges lodged by workers may also signal a growing dissatisfaction with union representation.[7] The litigation explosion under the NLRA has been so broad that a general analysis of behavioral responses to the regulatory framework provided by the NLRA is likely to be more revealing than an analysis of legal doctrine.

Unfair Labor Practices and Labor Relations Activity

One approach to explaining the growth of regulatory litigation is to view it as a more or less mechanical expansion of the activities subject to regulation. (Another approach, which views the expansion as the result of strategic interactions between labor, management, and the NLRB, is explored in chapter 5). Members of the NLRB often argue that the growth in the number of unfair labor practice charges is related to the expansion of the Board's jurisdiction brought about by the broadened industrial coverage of the act, by changes in economic activity

7. According to the Gallup poll, the proportion of union families approving of labor unions fell from 90 percent in 1965 to 73 percent in 1979. By 1985 the rate had risen to 81 percent. "Long Slide in Approval of Labor Unions Come to a Halt," *Gallup Report,* report 237 (June 1985), p. 30.

and inflation that have affected the regulatory system, and by expanded interpretations of the act by the Board and by the federal courts.[8] Each of these factors has contributed to the increase in regulatory activity, but they are not the main forces at work.

Industrial Jurisdiction

The industrial coverage of the NLRA has been expanded both by statute and by the Board's assertion of jurisdiction. The Postal Reorganization Act of 1970, for example, extended coverage of the NLRA to postal employees, a jurisdictional change that in the next ten years caused an increase of about 1,000 charges of unfair labor practices annually.[9] In 1970, the Board asserted jurisdiction over private, nonprofit colleges and universities with a gross annual revenue of at least $1 million,[10] which brought on about 100 additional charges per year.[11] In 1974, Congress eliminated the exemption of nonprofit hospitals from the act's coverage, and the NLRB subsequently accepted jurisdiction over proprietary hospitals and nursing homes that exceeded certain income thresholds.[12] Charges of unfair labor practices in these industries increased from 1,250 in fiscal 1974 to over 3,000 per year in the early 1980s.[13]

These increases in unfair labor practice charges represent only a small part of the general increase in regulatory litigation under the NLRA during the 1970s. In fiscal 1981, for example, some 5,000 to 6,000 charges may have been filed in industries over which the NLRB had acquired

8. Testimony of NLRB Chair Betty Southard Murphy, in *Oversight Hearings on the National Labor Relations Board,* Hearings before the Subcommittee on Labor-Management Relations of the House Committee on Education and Labor, 94 Cong. 1 sess. (GPO, 1976), p. 10; Testimony of NLRB Chair Donald L. Dotson, in *National Labor Relations Board Case Backlog,* Hearing before the Manpower and Housing Subcommittee of the House Committee on Government Operations, 98 Cong. 1 sess. (GPO, 1984), 2 vols.

9. The NLRB received 12,655 unfair labor practice charges pertaining to labor relations in the postal service between July 1, 1971, and September 30, 1982. Testimony of Dotson, in *NLRB Case Backlog,* Hearing, pt. 2, p. 75.

10. *Cornell University,* 183 N.L.R.B. 329 (1970).

11. Testimony of Murphy, in *Oversight Hearings,* p. 11.

12. *East Oakland Community Health Alliance, Inc.,* 218 N.L.R.B. 1270 (1975).

13. Testimony of Murphy, in *Oversight Hearings,* p. 10; *Annual Report of the National Labor Relations Board for the Fiscal Year Ended September 30, 1980, 1981,* and *1982,* table 5.

jurisdiction in the previous twenty years. But in 1981 there were 24,670 more charges filed than in fiscal 1969, just before the expansion in the NLRB's industrial jurisdiction occurred. The industries that were added to the Board's jurisdiction during the 1970s accounted at most for 20–25 percent of the increase in charges since 1969. Even this is likely to be an upper bound, however, since part of the net gain in charges in the expanded jurisdiction may reflect transfers of union resources from other covered jurisdictions.[14]

General Economic Forces

A different sort of jurisdictional issue links litigation under the NLRA with inflation. Although the jurisdiction of the NLRB in principle extends to "all enterprises whose operations 'affect' interstate or foreign commerce,"[15] the Board has discretion to limit its jurisdiction to enterprises that it believes have a substantial impact on commerce. In 1950, the Board began adopting nominal dollar standards for assuming jurisdiction in particular industries. Congress in 1959 confirmed the Board's authority to do so but also required the Board to accept all future cases that met the nominal dollar jurisdictional standards then in effect. Both NLRB members and outside observers have noted that inflation automatically expands the scope of the Board's activities, as more and more firms exceed the fixed-dollar standards.[16] How broad the effect of inflation is depends on the relation between the 1959 dollar standard and the distribution of firms by size in an industry. Data for examining this relation are elusive.[17] But for most industries the standards appear to

14. For example, unions probably would have allocated resources toward the health care industries, where they won 60 percent of the representation elections in 1975, and away from industries in which their victory rate was 50 percent.

15. *Annual Report of the NLRB for the Fiscal Year Ended September 30, 1980,* p. 27.

16. According to the statement submitted by Dotson, in *NLRB Case Backlog,* Hearing, pt. 2, p. 59, "the standard for retail stores is an annual sales volume of $500,000. Adjusting for inflation, an equivalent amount today is $1,400,000, using the 'GNP Deflator' series as a guide. Or, following the consumer price index, the equivalent would be at least $1,600,000 of business in 1983. This means that applying the $500,000 standard today is the equivalent of applying a standard of only $170,000 in 1959." See also Bernard D. Meltzer with Robert J. LaLonde, "Inflation and the NLRB," *Regulation,* vol. 4 (September–October 1980), pp. 43–45.

17. Meltzer with LaLonde, "Inflation and the NLRB," p. 44.

have been set so low that it is unlikely that there has been a large increase in the Board's jurisdiction as a result of this factor since 1970.[18]

Over the years, members of the NLRB have also conjectured that structural change in the economy can change the Board's caseload.[19] The development of new industry may be followed by union organizing activities that result in much regulatory litigation, and unfair labor practice charges may be used to protect job rights when plant closures are threatened. In periods of high unemployment, when bargaining power is relatively low, workers may prefer to substitute regulatory methods for collective bargaining as a means of improving working conditions.

The Link to Labor Relations Activities

The common theme in the jurisdictional and economic explanations of the growth in unfair labor practice charges is that the change depends on the volume of labor relations activity. The inadequacy of this line of explanation can be seen at a glance in figure 3-2. Variations in labor relations activity—here indexed by the annual number of representation elections, collective bargaining negotiations, and work stoppages— cannot explain the sharp increase in regulatory activity that has occurred since the late 1950s. By those measures, labor relations activity has been reasonably stable, while the number of unfair labor practice charges filed has accelerated rapidly.[20] That is, despite the extensions in the industrial

18. For example, the jurisdictional standard for nonretail establishments is purchases or sales of goods or services across state lines of at least $50,000 annually (established in *Siemons Mailing Service,* 122 N.L.R.B. 81 [1958]); for transit systems an annual gross volume of business of at least $250,000 (*Charleston Transit Co.,* 123 N.L.R.B. 1296 [1959]); for public utilities a gross annual volume of business of at least $250,000 or purchases or sales across state lines of at least $50,000 (*Sioux Valley Empire Electric Association,* 122 N.L.R.B. 92 [1958] and *Kingsbury Electric Cooperative, Inc.,* 138 N.L.R.B. 577 [1962]); and for newspaper companies publishing nationally syndicated features, advertising nationally sold products, or subscribing to an interstate news service a gross annual volume of at least $200,000 (*Belleville Employing Printers,* 122 N.L.R.B. 350 [1958]). Among the larger jurisdictional standards are gross annual revenue of at least $1 million for private nonprofit colleges and universities (29 C.F.R. 103.1 [1986]) and for symphony orchestras (29 C.F.R. 103.2 [1986]).

19. Testimony of Frank W. McCulloch, in *Departments of Labor and Health, Education, and Welfare Appropriations for 1965,* Hearings before the House Appropriations Committee, 88 Cong. 2 sess. (GPO, 1964); testimony of Murphy, in *Oversight Hearings,* p. 12.

20. The basic message of fig. 3-2 also emerges when different categories of charges or charges lodged by unions, employers, or individual workers are compared with measures of labor relations activity.

Figure 3-2. Charges of Unfair Labor Practices and Measures of Labor Relations Activity, 1948–80

Thousands

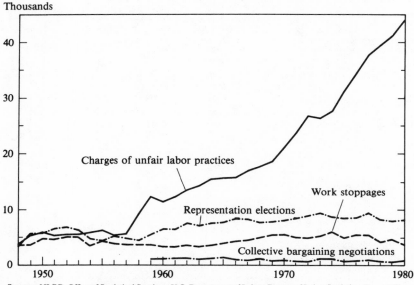

Sources: NLRB, Office of Statistical Services; U.S. Department of Labor, Bureau of Labor Statistics, *Current Wage Developments,* vol. 34 (February 1982), p. 17.

jurisdiction of the NLRB, there has been no marked increase in the total volume of labor relations activity subject to Board regulation. Therefore, the volume of activity in the industries traditionally covered by the NLRA must have declined as new jurisdictions were assumed. In any event, it is obvious from figure 3-2 that changes in the level of labor relations activity that resulted from the extension of the Board's industrial jurisdiction during the 1970s cannot explain a major portion of the growth of regulatory litigation.

The story is little changed when measures of inflation and unemployment are added to the analysis. The results of a multiple regression analysis for 1948–80 relating the annual number of unfair labor practice charges to measures of labor relations and economic activity are reported in table 3-3. The independent variables are the number of union representation elections, the number of work stoppages involving at least six workers, the civilian unemployment rate adjusted for changes in the demographic composition of the labor force, the rate of change of consumer prices, and a time trend.[21] Since the effects of changes in the

21. A continuous data series for the number of collective bargaining negotiations was not available for the period under study.

Table 3-3. Regressions of Charges of Unfair Labor Practices on Industrial Relations Activity and Economic Behavior in the United States, 1948–80

Variable	Regression number and estimation period[a]			
	1:1948–80	2:1948–80	3:1948–64	4:1965–80
Constant term	−27,515	−9,625	3,352	−12,460
	(4.30)	(2.01)	(0.42)	(0.58)
Representation elections, *ELEC*	4.48	0.49	2.25	4.22
	(6.50)	(0.67)	(4.71)	(1.38)
Work stoppages, *STOP*	−0.91	−0.08	−2.71	−3.31
	(0.65)	(0.09)	(2.22)	(1.50)
Unemployment rate, *UR*	2,845	1,461	661.97	2,687
	(3.68)	(2.79)	(0.85)	(2.01)
Rate of change of consumer prices, *CPI*	1,487	705	−48.65	1,615
	(5.59)	(3.49)	(0.18)	(3.50)
Time trend, *TIME*	. . .	904.5	. . .	. . .
		(6.73)		
Summary statistic				
$\bar{R}^{2}$ [b]	0.85	0.94	0.68	0.74
Durbin-Watson	1.05	0.82	1.94	1.12
Standard error of estimate	4,660	2,900	2,213	4,894

Sources: NLRB, Office of Statistical Services; George L. Perry, "Changing Labor Markets and Inflation," *Brookings Papers on Economic Activity, 3:1970,* pp. 411–41; U.S. Department of Labor, Bureau of Labor Statistics, *Current Wage Developments,* vol. 34 (February 1982), pp. 17–19; *Economic Report of the President, February 1984,* p. 283.

a. Regression coefficients and related test statistics are from regressions of the annual number of unfair labor practice charges, *ULP,* on the number of representation elections, *ELEC,* the number of work stoppages, *STOP,* the unemployment rate adjusted for demographic changes in the labor force, *UR,* the rate of change of the consumer price index, *CPI,* and a time trend, *TIME.* Numbers in parentheses are *t*-statistics.

b. Coefficient of determination adjusted for degrees of freedom.

NLRB's jurisdiction on labor relations activity will be captured, for example, by the elections variable, these regressions test the combined explanatory power of the jurisdiction, labor relations activity, and economic activity explanations.

Regression 1 indicates that unfair labor practice charges increase significantly with the number of union representation elections, the unemployment rate, and inflation, but that they are not significantly related to work stoppages.[22] If the effect of the level of labor relations activity on unfair labor practice charges increases as the rate of unemployment increases, then the regression specification of interaction should include the unemployment rate with elections and work stop-

22. These findings are consistent with those in Myron Roomkin, "A Quantitative Study of Unfair Labor Practice Cases," *Industrial and Labor Relations Review,* vol. 34 (January 1981), pp. 245–56.

pages. A test of this specification was not supportive, however.[23] Interpreting regression 1 literally, on average over the 1948–80 period, each representation election was associated with an increase of over 4 charges, a 1-percentage-point increase in the unemployment rate was associated with an increase of over 2,800 charges, and a 1-percentage-point increase in inflation was associated with an increase of almost 1,500 charges, after controlling for the effects of all other variables in the regression.

It can be treacherous to interpret such time series regressions literally, however. The very low Durbin-Watson statistics suggest the omission of important determinants of unfair labor practice charges from these regression specifications. In addition, unemployment and inflation rates and the number of charges of unfair labor practices were all considerably higher in the 1970s than in earlier periods, so that it is possible that the correlation shown in regression 1 in table 3-3 is the result of coincidence (and hence is spurious) rather than any causal connection between the variables. For example, when a simple time trend is added to the analysis (regression 2), neither measure of labor relations activity is significantly related to charges, and the coefficients on the measures of economic activity are cut in half. And when the sample period is split in half (regression 3), unemployment and inflation do not appear to have been significantly related to unfair labor practice charges during the 1948–64 period. The fact that they become statistically significant in the 1965–80 period (regression 4) may denote some influence of economic variables on regulatory litigation,[24] but the correlation may also occur because

23. For the period 1948–80, the estimated regression was

$$ULP = -20,575 - 2.01\,ELEC + 7.48\,STOP + 1.33\,UR^*ELEC - 1.32\,UR^*STOP.$$
$$\quad\quad (3.41)\quad (0.53)\quad\quad\quad (1.24)\quad\quad\quad (1.80)\quad\quad\quad\quad (1.14)$$

$\overline{R}^2 = 0.74$; Durbin-Watson statistic = 0.64; standard error of estimate = 6033

In this regression, ULP is the annual number of unfair labor practice charges filed, $ELEC$ the number of representation elections, $STOP$ the number of work stoppages, and UR the unemployment rate adjusted for demographic changes in the labor force; the numbers in parentheses are t-statistics; and $\overline{R}^2$ is the coefficient of determination adjusted for degrees of freedom. In other unreported regressions that explored the influence on regulatory litigation of business failures (used as a proxy for plant closings) and interacting economic and labor relations variables, none of the variables was significant.

24. The variances of the unemployment rate and the rate of change of consumer prices were smaller in the earlier period, so that it could have been more difficult to discern a true statistical relationship that may exist between these variables and unfair practice charges.

Figure 3-3. Charges of Unfair Labor Practices and Predictions Based on Three Models, 1965–80

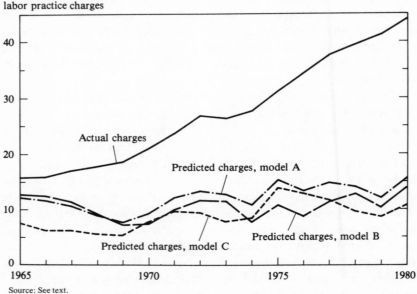

Thousands of unfair
labor practice charges

Source: See text.

charges increased during those years for completely independent reasons (as is apparent later, the latter interpretation is closer to the truth). When the sample is split into two periods, the relationship increases from 2 charges per election in the first period to 4 charges in the second, but the effect of the elections variable is measured much less precisely in the second period. The same can be said of the work stoppages variable, which also has an unexpected negative coefficient in both periods.

The incorporation of economic variables in the analysis of unfair labor practice charges does not explain the puzzling gap between the levels of litigation and labor relations activity under the NLRA. This is demonstrated in figure 3-3, which shows the actual number of charges and the number predicted by three models using different sets of variables. When model A, a regression relating unfair labor practice charges to both labor relations and economic behavior for the period 1948–64 (regression 3 in table 3-3) is used to predict the behavior of unfair practice charges for 1965–80, the predictions fall short throughout the period. Beginning in the third year of the prediction period (1967), the actual number of charges exceeds the upper bound of the 5 percent confidence interval around the predictions. By the last five years of the prediction period, the prediction error is over twice the size of the predicted number of unfair labor practice charges.[25]

When the explanatory variables in figure 3-3 are limited solely to measures of labor relations activity, model B underpredicts substantially. By 1976–80 the prediction error is two to three times the predicted value of unfair labor practice charges. When only economic variables are used to predict the path of regulatory activity, in model C, errors are even more extreme. Prediction errors fall outside the 5 percent confidence interval beginning in the first year of the prediction period. Moreover, model C predicts a decline in unfair practice charges over 1975–79, largely because the coefficient on the rate of change of consumer prices (which increased substantially during this period, while unemployment fell) is negative in the 1948–64 predicting equation. Clearly, the models depicted in figure 3-3 do not explain the growth of regulatory litigation under the NLRA. Nor do models that narrow the particular areas of the NLRA or the relationship between unions, employers, and the NLRB. In every statutory category of unfair labor practice, models relating charges to labor relations behavior and economic developments underpredict the volume of unfair labor practice charges throughout the 1970s. The same is true when charges by unions, by employers, and by individual workers are examined separately. Again the impression is that the explosion of litigation under the NLRA reflects general behavioral factors influencing the parties to labor relations rather than the consequences of a particular decision or doctrine.

These results and the conclusions that flow from them rest to an important extent on the assumption that the measures of labor relations activity used in the analysis adequately capture changes in the activities that are subject to regulation. The accuracy of the analysis of union organizing activity is particularly important, since it is a major source of regulatory litigation. If union organizing activity has increased substantially, but the fraction of organizing efforts resulting in representation elections has declined, the observed elections used to index organizing

25. Because the coefficient on the variable for changes in consumer prices is very small relative to the coefficient on the unemployment rate for the 1948–64 sample period, the predicted number of unfair practice charges actually declines (contrary to the actual behavior of these charges) during the late 1960s and late 1970s. The predicted number for 1980 is little more than the predicted number for 1975, whereas the actual number is 40 percent higher.

activity in the empirical analysis would understate the actual amount of activity. But figure 3-2 illustrates that the annual number of representation elections was relatively stable over the period under study. Therefore, any increase in the ratio of organizing attempts to representation elections would be reflected as an increase in organizing activity since the late 1950s. The best evidence available indicates that there has been little if any increase in real organizing expenditures per unorganized production worker during this period.[26]

Comparison with Canada and Japan

Is the growing gap between regulatory activity and labor relations activity an inherent feature of regulation that follows the NLRA model, or does it reflect idiosyncrasies in either the administration of or the response of the parties to the regulatory scheme? Only two other countries—Canada and Japan—have adopted a similar public policy toward labor relations. Policy in Canada is closest to the regulatory structure in the United States.

The constitutional division of authority in Canada leaves most issues of public policy toward labor relations in the jurisdiction of the provinces, whose regulatory approaches usually follow those of the NLRA. For example, the Labour Relations Act of the Province of Ontario resembles the NLRA in most important respects. The act establishes the Ontario Labour Relations Board (OLRB) and makes it responsible for certifying labor unions as collective bargaining agents, investigating "complaints of contraventions of the Act" (unfair labor practices), issuing remedial orders where the complaints are sustained, terminating bargaining rights,

26. After a careful construction and analysis of the organizing expenditures of twenty national unions (representing half of all union members), Paula B. Voos, "Trends in Union Organizing Expenditures, 1953–1977," *Industrial and Labor Relations Review,* vol. 38 (October 1984), p. 60, concludes that "the best of the imperfect measures available of organizing expenditures show that in 1974 they were about the same relative to the target population of potentially organizable workers as in 1953." The Voos data also reveal a distinct drop in real organizing expenditures per unorganized production worker from 1969 to 1974. In order to determine whether representation elections have provided an increasingly unreliable indication of union organizing activity, Voos's two measures of real organizing expenditures per unorganized production worker were regressed on the number of elections and a time trend. A significantly positive time trend would confirm a growth in organizing activity relative to representation elections. For one measure of organizing expenditures, the time trend was insignificant; for the other, it indicated a significant increase of real organizing expenditures per unorganized worker of about one penny per year!

issuing declarations where unlawful strikes or lockouts have occurred, and settling jurisdictional disputes arising out of the assignment of work.[27]

The specific unfair labor practices that the OLRB investigates and adjudicates generally resemble those in the NLRA. Under the Labour Relations Act, it is illegal for employers to interfere with employees exercising their right to form and join trade unions, to contribute financial or other support to a trade union, to discriminate against employees because of their membership in or support of a union, to bargain with a union that is not the certified bargaining agent of the workers, to use strikebreakers, or to refuse to bargain in good faith. It is also illegal under the act for unions to assist, support, or interfere with the formation of an employer's organization, to attempt to interfere with the bargaining rights of a certified union, to fail to represent members fairly, or to fail to allocate employment and other economic opportunities in a fair manner.[28] The system of adjudication is quite similar to the system in the United States under the NLRA, with the exception that the scope for judicial review of the Ontario Labour Relations Board's decisions is so limited that decisions seldom can be appealed to the federal courts.

Data collected in the administration of the Ontario law permit some comparison with the U.S. experience under the NLRA. The growth of unfair labor practice charges filed with the OLRB since 1965 resembles the pattern of growth in the United States except in timing (figure 3-4). After a period of relatively slow growth (about 6 percent per year) during 1965–74, there was a sharp increase in the growth of charges of unfair labor practice filed with the OLRB. Since 1974, such charges have increased at a rate of over 18 percent per year.

Although the unfair labor practices established in U.S. and Ontarian law are quite similar, almost no charges are filed by employers under Ontario's law. Data from the mid-1970s indicate that 60–65 percent of the charges are filed by unions against employers—usually alleging discrimination against workers because of their union activities, illegal changes in employment conditions, and failure to bargain in good faith—while virtually all of the remaining charges are filed by individual workers against unions or against unions and employers jointly. Most of the

27. The OLRB also has special functions pertaining to labor relations in the construction industry that have no direct parallel in the United States.
28. Government of Ontario, *Labour Relations Act* (Toronto: Queen's Printer for Ontario, 1984).

Figure 3-4. Charges of Unfair Labor Practices, Ontario, Canada, 1965–83

Unfair labor practice charges

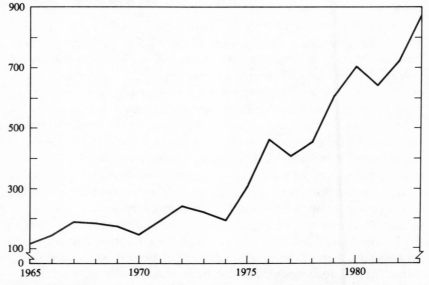

Sources: Ontario Ministry of Labour, *Annual Report,* various years; Ontario Labour Relations Board, *Annual Report,* various years.

charges by workers allege violations of the union's duty to represent them fairly in grievances against employers.[29]

As in the United States, regulatory officials tend to associate the increase in unfair practice charges with increases in activity surrounding the certification of unions. In order to determine whether the sharp acceleration in unfair labor practice charges under the Ontario Labour Relations Act since 1974 could be attributed to an increase in the labor relations activity that is subject to regulation, time series regressions relating charges of unfair practices to the number of applications for certification of bargaining agents, the number of representation elections held, and the number of expirations of collective bargaining agreements were estimated for various periods since 1965 for which data were available. If there is a stable relationship between unfair practice charges and labor relations activity in Ontario, these variables should be positively and significantly related to the number of charges filed. (A time trend was included in some of the regressions to determine whether the

29. Ontario Ministry of Labour, *Annual Report, 1973/74, 1974/75,* and *1975/76.*

Table 3-4. Regressions of Charges of Unfair Labor Practices on Industrial Relations Activity in Ontario, Canada, 1968–83

Variable	Regression number and estimation period[a]			
	1:1968–83	2:1968–83	3:1973–83	4:1973–83
Constant term	1,513.8	375.3	915.0	188.1
	(2.13)	(1.46)	(1.99)	(1.04)
Certification applications	−0.749	−0.261	. . .	. . .
	(1.77)	(1.79)		
Expiration of agreements	−0.099	−0.022	0.086	0.006
	(0.83)	(0.56)	(0.79)	(0.16)
Representation elections	. . .	. . .	−2.98	−0.30
			(2.26)	(0.55)
Time trend	. . .	44.77	. . .	61.57
		(10.46)		(7.95)
Summary statistic				
$\bar{R}^2$ [b]	0.07	0.90	0.29	0.92
Durbin-Watson	0.45	1.65	0.51	2.26
Standard error of estimate	229	75	185	62

Sources: Ontario Ministry of Labour, *Annual Report,* various years; Ontario Labour Relations Board, *Annual Report,* various years; Ontario Ministry of Labour, Research Branch, *Ontario Collective Bargaining Agreement Expirations,* various years.

a. Regression coefficients and test statistics are from regressions of the annual number of unfair labor practice charges on the number of applications for certification of bargaining agents, the number of expiring collective bargaining agreements, and a time trend. In regressions for 1973–83, the number of representation elections was substituted for the number of applications for certification. Numbers in parentheses are t-statistics.

b. Coefficients of determination adjusted for degrees of freedom.

number of charges grew independently of variations in labor relations activity.)

Table 3-4 shows that for each of the time periods and specifications, measures of labor relations activity were either not significantly related to unfair practice charges or, contrary to expectation, were negatively related to charges. When the time trend was added to a regression, it dominated the results—just as in the analysis of the U.S. data. The Canadian data reveal the same acceleration of charges and the absence of the connection between regulatory activity and labor relations activity stressed in most official explanations of the phenomenon. More generally, the parallel finding in the Canadian data suggests that the basic empirical puzzle is not related to idiosyncratic aspects of the administration of the NLRA but may instead be rooted in behavioral responses to the particular approach to regulation of labor relations adopted in both countries.

The Japanese regulation of labor relations, although established during the postwar American occupation and based on the U.S. model, resembles the NLRA much less than Canadian policy does. Given the differences from North American policy, the different outcomes are instructive. Japanese statutes proscribe certain practices by employers and assign to an administrative agency, the Labor Relations Commission (and forty-seven local labor commissions), the responsibility for the implementation of Japanese labor relations regulations.[30] However, the rights to organize labor unions and to bargain collectively are constitutionally guaranteed in Japan, and Japanese law does not provide for representation elections and the associated regulatory apparatus as a means of establishing union representation. The notion of exclusive representation is therefore unknown in Japan (and most countries outside of North America), and the Labor Relations Commission has no role in determining the appropriate units for collective bargaining. Without elections and with no unfair practices by unions specified in statutes, Japan has fewer sources of unfair labor practice charges than the United States and Canada. Within the limitations of a three-country comparison, it does appear that the regulation of representation elections is a central factor in the volume of charges filed. In Japan, where the process of organizing unions is not regulated, about 1,000 new charges of unfair practice are filed each year, whereas 25,000–30,000 charges are filed against employers annually in the United States and over 600 a year were filed in Ontario in the late 1970s. Moreover, Japan has not experienced the sharp growth in charges observed in North America in recent decades.[31]

The analysis of U.S. and Canadian data undermines the hypothesis that the growth of regulatory litigation is a more or less mechanical extension of the spread of regulatory jurisdiction over time. Of the various activities that might be influenced by NLRA-style regulation, only union representation elections bear some systematic statistical relation to unfair labor practice charges, and even this relationship appears to have weakened since the mid-1960s in the United States and was not even discernible in the data for Ontario, Canada. Of central importance is the fact that the statistical relationship between elections and charges found in the U.S. data, even when augmented by data on

30. The commissions also are responsible for resolving disputes and thus combine the functions of the NLRB and the Federal Mediation and Conciliation Service in the United States.

31. For example, the number of new charges filed was 1,022 in 1975, 749 in 1978, and 862 in 1980. William B. Gould, *Japan's Reshaping of American Labor Law* (MIT Press, 1984), p. 48; chap. 2 discusses the differences between Japanese and U.S. labor law.

economic activity, explains very little of the acceleration in charges that began in the late 1950s. The key to this regulatory puzzle must be found in explanations of why a given level of labor relations activity gave rise to four times as many unfair practice charges in 1980 as twenty years earlier.

Shifts within Industries and Regions

The central fact that unfair labor practice charges have risen relative to regulated labor relations activity may simply reflect shifts in the distribution of labor relations activity from sectors with a low likelihood of employer resistance to sectors with a high likelihood. (Factors contributing to a growth in regulatory litigation in all sectors are analyzed in chapter 5.)

Unions will rationally attempt to establish collective bargaining relationships first in regions and industries where employees seem most amenable to union formation and employer resistance is low. As unions move on to more difficult targets, resistance to unionization will be greater and failure to comply with NLRA regulations more likely. Unfair labor practice charges may therefore increase over time as unions move on to industries and regions that are progressively more difficult to organize. Shifts in the distribution of labor relations activity would then explain rising charges. This "selectivity" argument rests on the notion that the growth in regulatory litigation will reflect a shift in the distribution of labor relations activity from regions or industries where the likelihood of a charge is relatively low to regions or industries where the likelihood of a charge is high. Within each sector, however, there will be no change over time in the likelihood that labor relations activity will generate unfair practice charges.

The explanatory power of this argument can be explored through application of the simple accounting identity

$$(1) \qquad ULP^t \equiv \sum_{i=1}^{n} \left(ULP_i^t \Big/ A_i^t \right) \left(A_i^t \right)$$

in which the volume of unfair labor practice charges ULP in year t is defined as the level of labor relations activity A in sector i in year t times the ratio of charges to activity in that sector ULP_i^t/A_i^t, summed across all sectors n. This latter term indicates the frequency with which unfair labor practice charges result from labor relations activity. A necessary condition for the selectivity argument to have merit is that this ratio vary across sectors, so that unfair labor practice charges can increase from shifts in the distribution of labor relations activities from sectors in which the ratio is low to sectors in which the ratio is high.

Taking the derivative of equation 1 with respect to time yields a common decomposition of changes in the number of unfair labor practice charges:

$$
(2) \quad \mathrm{d}ULP^t/\mathrm{d}t = \sum_{i=1}^{n} \left(ULP_i^t \Big/ A_i^t \right) \left(\mathrm{d}A_i \right)
$$

$$
+ \sum_{i=1}^{n} \left[A_i^t \right] \left[\mathrm{d}(ULP_i \Big/ A_i) \right] + \sum_{i=1}^{n} \left[\mathrm{d}A_i \right] \left[\mathrm{d}(ULP_i \Big/ A_i) \right].
$$

If structural change in the distribution of labor relations activity (the selectivity argument) is the sole reason for the growth of regulatory litigation, the entire increase in unfair labor practice charges would be explained by the first term on the right-hand side of equation 2. In this term, the ratio of charges to activity in each sector is held constant, allowing changes in the distribution of activity across sectors to change total litigation. However, if the assumption of constant frequency ratios ULP_i/A_i is invalid, as would be the case with shifts in the degree of compliance with the law, changes in the volume of regulatory litigation would occur even when there was no effect from structural change. This effect is captured by the second term on the right-hand side of equation 2. The interaction between changes in activity and changes in the frequency ratios across sectors is captured by the final term.

Table 3-5 presents the results of an empirical examination of the role that the changing distribution of labor relations activity plays in the growth of charges.[32] Representation elections, one of the major sources of unfair labor practice charges, are used to capture possible violations of the act against workers who are not yet unionized. Union membership, a broad measure of the scope of representation, represents the potential

---

32. An "ideal" application of the decomposition approach to this problem would have used multivariate analysis of unfair labor practice charges with representation elections or some other measure of labor relations activity as the unit of observation. Unfortunately there was no practical way to match information on labor relations activity with information on regulatory litigation at a disaggregated level.

Table 3-5. Effects of Changes in the Distribution of Labor Relations Activity by Region and Industry on Charges Filed, 1960–70 and 1970–80

Percent

Increase in charges explained by	Measure of labor relations activity			
	Representation elections		Union membership	
	1960–70	1970–80	1960–70	1970–80
Regional structure				
Changes across all regions	31	1	50	14
Changes within regions	54	97	35	74
Interaction of changes across and within regions	14	2	15	12
Total[a]	100	100	100	100
Industrial structure				
Changes across all industries	31	1	9	0
Changes within industries	54	62	84	100
Interaction of changes across and within industries	14	37	7	0
Total[a]	100	100	100	100

Sources: *Annual Report of the National Labor Relations Board for the Fiscal Year Ended June 30, 1960* and *1970* and *September 30, 1980*, table 5; Bureau of Labor Statistics, *Directory of National and International Labor Unions in the United States, 1961*, bulletin 1320 (Government Printing Office, 1962), table 8, and *Directory of National Unions and Employee Associations, 1971*, bulletin 1750 (GPO, 1972), table 17; Courtney D. Gifford, ed., *Directory of U.S. Labor Organizations, 1982–83* (Washington: Bureau of National Affairs, 1982), table 14.

a. Totals may not add to 100 because of rounding.

for violations of the act as it pertains to organized workers (unfortunately, this measure does not directly represent specific activities that are subject to regulation). The results of the analysis for changes in the volume of charges during 1960–70 and 1970–80 are reported in table 3-5; the three rows of results under regional structure and industrial structure refer respectively to the three terms on the right-hand side of equation 2.

By either measure, there has been scope for unfair labor practice charges to increase as a result of a regional redistribution of labor relations activity over time. In both 1960 and 1970, the likelihood of an unfair practice charge in some regions was two to three times the likelihood in other regions.[33] If selectivity along regional dimensions

33. In 1960, for example, the ratio of charges to union members ranged from 0.0005 in New England to 0.0017 in the South Atlantic region, and the ratio of charges to representation elections varied from 1.15 in the West North Central region to 2.26 in the Middle Atlantic region. In 1970 the ratio of charges to union members ranged from 0.07 in New England to 0.18 in the Mountain states, while the number of charges per

were the sole factor, the increase of 9,681 unfair labor practice charges per year between 1960 and 1970 and the increase of 23,025 charges per year between 1970 and 1980 would be the result of changes in the regional distribution of representation elections and union membership. The changes that did occur during the 1960s on balance reallocated union membership and representation elections toward regions that had relatively high probabilities of unfair practice charges in 1960, thereby tending to raise the number of unfair practice charges resulting from a given level of labor relations activity. Nevertheless, changes in the structure of labor relations activity across all regions could only explain one-third to one-half of the growth of regulatory litigation (table 3-5). That is, during the 1960s, the increase in the annual number of charges filed was about three times the growth predicted on the basis of the changing pattern of elections and twice the growth predicted on the basis of the changing distribution of union membership. And increases in the frequency of charges within regions were a roughly equivalent source of change.

The story is even more dramatic between 1970 and 1980, when the annual number of unfair labor practice charges filed effectively doubled, to 44,063. Although changes in the distribution of labor relations activity during the 1970s were again toward regions with relatively high likelihoods of unfair practice charges, the effect on the total number of charges filed was even smaller than in the 1960s. The proportion of the increase in charges from 1970 to 1980 attributable to the selectivity idea range from 1 percent under the representation election measure of labor relations activity to 14 percent under the union membership measure. It is clear that it was the increased frequency of unfair labor practice filings within regions rather than a structural change in the distribution of labor relations activity that was the major source of growth in regulatory litigation under the NLRA during the 1970s, accounting for between 74 percent and 97 percent of the change!

The data therefore do not support the idea that rising charges are

---

representation election ranged from 1.78 in New England to 3.25 in the Middle Atlantic states. *Annual Report of the NLRB for the Fiscal Year Ended June 30, 1960* and *1970* and *September 30, 1980*, table 5; Bureau of Labor Statistics, *Directory of National and International Labor Unions in the United States, 1961*, bulletin 1320 (Government Printing Office, 1962), table 8, and *Directory of National Unions and Employee Associations, 1971*, bulletin 1750 (GPO, 1972), table 17; Courtney D. Gifford, ed., *Directory of U.S. Labor Organizations, 1982–83* (Washington: BNA, 1983), table 14.

mainly the result of regional pockets of resistance to unionism. While there have always been some regional differences in the likelihood of a charge being filed—the selectivity argument is based precisely on the existence of such differences—the upward shift in the ratio of unfair labor practice charges to labor relations activity is across the board, irrespective of the measure of labor relations activity used.

The results of an analysis by industry are parallel to the regional results. Over the same two decades, the likelihood that an unfair labor practice charge would be filed varied across industries by a factor of at least 10, providing considerable scope for an effect from structural change.[34] The relatively modest changes in the industrial distribution of representation elections and union membership that occurred during the 1960s on balance reallocated labor relations activity toward industries that had relatively high probabilities of unfair labor practice charges, but these changes accounted for even less of the increasing litigation during the 1960s than the changing regional distribution of labor relations activity. An increasing likelihood that labor relations activities within industries would result in unfair practice charges was a more important source of the growth of litigation.

During the 1970s, the distribution of union membership shifted somewhat from the smokestack industries, where organization was initially strongest, toward the services. The remarkable fact is that, according to the industry analysis, essentially none of the growth of unfair labor practice charges can be accounted for by interindustry shifts in the distribution of labor relations activity. Instead, for each industry, the ratio of unfair labor practice charges to labor relations activity rose even more dramatically than it had in the 1960s (and by the membership measure accounted for all of the increase during the 1970s).

Although the measures reported in table 3-5 are rough (given the barriers to controlling for the effects of several influences simultaneously) and the exact values in the decomposition analysis therefore vary with the measure of labor relations activity, the analysis does help to narrow the puzzle. Very little of the rise in charges of unfair labor

34. In 1960 the ratio of unfair practice charges to union membership ranged from 0.0002 in the communications industry to 0.002 in trade, while the ratio of charges to representation elections varied from 1.1 in trade and communications to 16.5 in construction. In 1970 the ratio of charges to membership ranged from 0.007 in communications and mining to 0.03 in finance and the ratio of charges to elections from 1.6 in finance to 16.5 in construction. Ibid.

practices, particularly during the 1970s, can be explained by changes in the regional and industrial distribution of labor relations activity. What is needed is an explanation of the general growth of unfair labor practice charges in all regions and all industries.

The Breadth of Change

A striking feature of the growing volume of litigation associated with the regulation of labor relations under the NLRA is its breadth. With charges of unfair labor practices rising in every category of the law and among all parties to labor relations, it seems unlikely that the growth of litigation can be traced to a few key changes in legal doctrine under the act. Very little of the growth can be explained by changes in the volume of labor relations activity (including growth resulting from the expansion of the NLRB's jurisdiction over time), the regional and industrial distribution of labor relations activities, unemployment, and inflation. The central puzzle is why the amount of litigation arising from a given level of labor relations activity has increased so much since the late 1950s.

Some critics suggest that it reflects a surge of frivolous litigation, initiated by the parties as a low-cost harassment tactic within the general adversarial relationship between unions and management. The facts do not support this argument, however. When a charge of unfair practice is initially filed, a regional office of the NLRB makes a judgment as to the merit of the charge. To attribute the growth in charges to an explosion of frivolous regulatory litigation implies that a declining proportion of unfair labor practice charges would have sufficient merit to warrant issuance of complaints by the NLRB. During the 1970s, 32.4 percent of the charges filed were found by the Board to have merit—essentially the same as the 32.8 percent found to have merit in the 1960s.[35]

Instead, the empirical puzzle developed in this chapter must reflect behavioral responses of the parties to the regulatory system. Thus the next two chapters trace the incentives of the parties to use the regulatory system strategically. Chapter 4 reviews evidence on the apparent impact of NLRB regulation, and chapter 5 analyzes the nature of the compliance and monitoring game played by parties subject to the NLRA as the

35. Those found to have merit in the 1950s, before the acceleration of charges, were 26.9 percent. Data provided by NLRB, Office of Statistical Services.

structure of compliance incentives changes. The importance of understanding these behavioral responses is underscored by the fact that Canadian experience indicates that the growing gap between regulatory litigation and labor relations activity may be a general characteristic of systems of regulation that are modeled on the NLRA.

CHAPTER 4

NLRB Regulation and Labor Relations Outcomes

AT ABOUT the time when litigation under the National Labor Relations Act began to accelerate, union representation in the private sector in the United States began a sustained decline. Union membership peaked at about 35 percent of the nonagricultural work force in 1955 and declined to about 18 percent in 1984. The decline in representation of private-sector workers has been only partially offset by the surge of unionization in the public sector since the early 1960s.

It is generally recognized that the decline is not solely the result of the growth of litigation under the NLRA. Nevertheless, the exact effect of NLRA regulation and the associated litigation on union representation and other labor relations outcomes has been a matter of controversy, in part because these outcomes also depend on nonregulatory factors and in part because there is considerable dispute over how specific doctrinal rulings of the National Labor Relations Board affect labor relations.

This chapter examines the relationship between unfair labor practices and labor relations outcomes in order to judge how the regulation of labor relations has contributed to the decline of unions. An understanding of this relationship is also important to determine whether public regulatory resources are being used efficiently to realize the objectives of or rights guaranteed by the NLRA. Beyond that, this chapter attempts to gain some insight into the incentives for compliance and noncompliance with the act.

Studies of the impact of the act seek to delineate the difference between labor relations outcomes under the law and what would have occurred in the absence of the law. The central question is whether the labor practices that the statute prohibits have any impact on the outcomes. If they do not, then regulation of the behavior should be irrelevant for the outcomes, and there should be little incentive to violate the law. If regulation is directed at behavior that can alter outcomes, however, then there are inherent incentives for noncompliance, and the entire issue of compliance choices has a bearing on the outcome of regulatory policy.

These considerations raise two methodological issues. How is the outcome that would have occurred in the absence of the NLRA to be specified? And how is the choice of whether or not to use a regulatory procedure to be handled? Estimates of regulatory impact will in general depend on whether the statistical procedures used allow for the fact that use of the regulatory system is only one of the means that the parties to collective bargaining might choose to obtain their objectives. The decision to use NLRA regulatory procedures rather than alternative means such as negotiations and work stoppages may itself be revealing information on the outcomes that would be likely in the absence of the statute. This chapter begins by assessing the findings of regulatory impact of the NLRB. The larger issue of employer resistance and the general level of union representation in the economy is then analyzed.

The Outcome of Union Representation Elections

The effect of unfair labor practices on the outcome of union representation elections has been extensively debated by academics and practitioners because of the potential connection between election outcomes and the general coverage of labor unions. The proportion of elections won by unions in the United States has steadily declined during the years that charges of unfair labor practice have accelerated (see figure 4-1). Over the same period there has also been an increase in the number of decertification elections held, and the proportion of these elections won by unions has decreased.[1] One side in the extended debate among academic observers and practitioners has attributed the decline in union membership to the decline in election victories, which in turn is a result of increasing unfair labor practices. (Decertification elections are often mentioned in these arguments, but the numbers involved are too small to be of much consequence.[2])

1. National Labor Relations Board, Office of Statistical Services, data for 1948–80.
2. The AFL-CIO does not adhere to such a simple explanation; it attributes some

Figure 4-1. Percent of Representation Elections Won by Unions, 1948–80

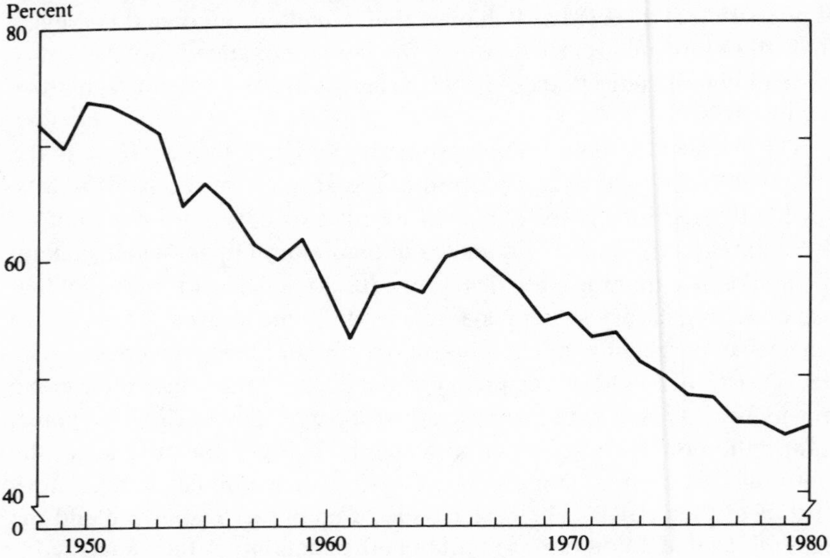

Percent

Source: National Labor Relations Board, Office of Statistical Services.

The chain of attribution raises two questions. To what extent does union coverage of the work force depend on the proportion of elections won? And to what extent is union success in representation elections influenced by employers' unfair labor practices?

Election Success and Union Coverage

While the percentage of the work force represented by unions has been declining since the mid-1950s, even the absolute number of union members has been falling since 1978. Union election fortunes, of course, do not wholly account for these trends. Membership varies with cyclical or secular changes in the employment level at organized plants with union shop arrangements, with plant closures, and (for a given success rate) with the intensity of union organizing activity.

To a certain extent, the decline in unionization reflects an apparent

of its membership decline to changes in the industrial and geographic structure of employment and a decline in the proportion of the work force in traditional full-time, full-year working patterns. See AFL-CIO Committee on the Evolution of Work, *The Changing Situation of Workers and Their Unions* (Washington: AFL-CIO, 1985), pp. 8–11.

reduction in organizing activity by unions. About 3 percent of nonunion labor was involved in certification elections in 1950 and less than 1 percent in 1980. Most of the decline occurred rather precipitously in the 1950s, but the decline continued through the 1970s.[3] Unions also had a falling success rate in elections during the period (figure 4-1). These facts could easily reflect a decision by unions to organize first bargaining units where their probability of success is highest (given employee attitudes toward union representation) and later proceed to more difficult situations. As the cost per organizing effort would rise over time, it is hardly surprising that the resources allocated to organizing activity declined.

Nonetheless, the effect of economic factors—employment and labor force growth—accounts for a large amount of the reduced coverage of unions. Dickens and Leonard estimate that if the net growth attributable to economic factors had remained at its 1950 level, the portion of employed workers who were union members would have been 32 percent higher in 1980. Economic factors had a particularly strong effect on the declining coverage of unions during the 1970s, when concern about the role of employers' unfair labor practices increased. If the union success rate in elections had remained at its level in the early 1950s (about 75 percent), unions would have represented 25 percent of non-agricultural wage and salary workers in 1980 (rather than the 21 percent they actually represented). Similarly, if the organization rate had remained constant at the level of the early 1950s, unions would have represented 27 percent of the work force. The two factors do not act independently, however, and as it turns out, only if both the organizing rate and the success rate in elections remained at their levels of the early 1950s would union coverage in the early 1980s be close to what it was in the 1950s.[4]

Less than a fifth of the decline in proportionate union representation since the early 1950s can be attributed directly to the decline in union election success. Lower election success may have an additional indirect influence on unionization by reducing the resources allocated to organizing activity, but for this interaction to explain virtually all of the

3. William T. Dickens and Jonathan S. Leonard, "Accounting for the Decline in Union Membership, 1950–1980," *Industrial and Labor Relations Review,* vol. 38 (April 1985), pp. 323–34.

4. Ibid., pp. 329–34. See also Albert Rees, "The Size of Union Membership in Manufacturing in the 1980s," in Hervey A. Juris and Myron Roomkin, eds., *The Shrinking Perimeter: Unionism and Labor Relations in the Manufacturing Sector* (Lexington Books, 1980), pp. 43–53.

decline in union representation since the early 1950s, the decline in union election success would have to account for all of the decline in organizing activity. Moreover, all of the decline in election success would have to be the result of illegal acts by employers.

Unfair Labor Practices and Election Success

About one-third of the unfair labor practice charges filed under the NLRA are related to representation elections. In order to determine the influence of violations of the NLRA on the outcomes of union elections, it is necessary to know what determines how workers vote in representation elections and whether voting intentions are altered by the behavior that the NLRB regulates in its administration of the unfair labor practice provisions.

Many empirical models of election outcomes are structured as if regulated campaign activities are the only factor at work in determining how individual employees vote on union representation; they implicitly assume that there is no regularity in employee voting behavior in the absence of federal regulation. Other models ignore completely the potential influences of NLRB regulation on the union representation choices over the past fifty years.

STUDIES OF UNION MEMBERSHIP. The most broadly focused studies of unionization attempt to explain the stock of union members in an industry as a fraction of the level of employment or the labor force in the industry. But they do not isolate what influence the choices—such as whether to vote for union representation—presented under NLRA regulations might have on unionization. What they describe is the net outcome of those choices plus other factors.

These broad studies reveal substantial variations in union membership by industry, region, and demographic group. In 1980, union representation of blue-collar wage and salary workers varied from 62 percent in transportation to around 21 percent in retail trade, finance, and services. Traditionally, union coverage has been lowest in the South; nonwhites have been more likely than whites to be union members; and college graduates have been less likely than others to join unions.[5] These

5. Bureau of Labor Statistics, *Earnings and Other Characteristics of Organized Workers, May 1980,* bulletin 2105 (Government Printing Office, 1981), table 15; Harry J. Holzer, "Unions and the Labor Market Status of White and Minority Youth," *Industrial and Labor Relations Review,* vol. 35 (April 1982), pp. 392–405; Courtney D. Gifford, ed., *Directory of U.S. Labor Organizations, 1982–83* (Washington: Bureau of National Affairs, 1982), table 21.

variations in union penetration are not generally attributed to differences in the degree of employer resistance to unionism but to more fundamental factors that have an uneven incidence across industries, regions, and demographic groups. Concentrated industries in which organized employees have a chance of capturing a share of excess profits tend to have high unionization rates (even though these same profits might provide employers with more resources with which to resist unions).[6] The economies of scale in union organizing are seen in the fact that unionized establishments have larger numbers of employees than nonunion establishments. Capital-intensity in production is also associated with higher levels of unionization, apparently because the technology leaves workers with less discretion over their work schedules.[7] Workers in jobs with more structured work settings, greater safety hazards, less flexible hours of work, faster work paces, and less employee control over the assignment of overtime hours are also more likely to be union members.[8]

Of the patterns noted, only the lower degree of unionization in the South may be extensively related to opposition to unions, and because some of that reflects general community resistance, it is beyond the reach of the NLRA (if it is not traceable to an employer's actions). The general impression created by evidence in the broad studies is that many factors other than employer campaign tactics determine the pattern of union representation. In order to ascertain whether the factors that govern unionization in general also apply to the outcomes of elections brought under NLRA regulations, it is necessary to determine what effects employer campaign tactics have on voting behavior in union elections.

STUDIES OF EMPLOYEE VOTING BEHAVIOR. A careful study of the effect of illegal labor relations activities on voting in union representation elections should provide a model of the general determinants of voting in an environment without regulation (where employees make their

---

6. Leonard W. Weiss, "Concentration and Labor Earnings," *American Economic Review,* vol. 56 (March 1966), pp. 96–117; Orley Ashenfelter and George E. Johnson, "Unionism, Relative Wages, and Labor Quality in U.S. Manufacturing Industries," *International Economic Review,* vol. 13 (October 1972), pp. 488–508.

7. Daniel J. B. Mitchell, *Unions, Wages, and Inflation* (Brookings, 1980), p. 84.

8. Greg J. Duncan and Frank P. Stafford, "Do Union Members Receive Compensating Wage Differentials?" *American Economic Review,* vol. 70 (June 1980), pp. 355–71; J. Paul Leigh, "Are Unionized Blue Collar Jobs More Hazardous than Nonunionized Blue Collar Jobs?" *Journal of Labor Research,* vol. 3 (Summer 1982), pp. 349–57; Ronald G. Ehrenberg and Paul L. Schumann, *Longer Hours or More Jobs?* (Ithaca, N.Y.: ILR Press, 1982), chap. 7.

choice regarding representation in an election with no campaign activity). Such a model should recognize that factors other than activities regulated under the NLRA may influence the union representation choice in order to avoid attributing to campaign behavior effects that in fact have much deeper behavioral roots. This approach would in essence provide information on the determinants of worker choice if union representation elections were held immediately after a petition for an election is filed with the NLRB.[9] (A proposal for "instant" representation elections is discussed in chapter 6.) In addition, it should address how the choice of union representation would be altered by illegal campaign activity. Few studies of union elections address both issues, and those that do usually use indirect measures such as charges of unfair labor practices to represent illegal activity (largely because they are easier to observe than actual illegal activity).

Several studies in the organizational behavior literature have focused on the general determinants of voting by individual workers.[10] Using a variety of samples of white-collar and blue-collar workers in several industries, these studies find uniformly that there is an inverse relation between aspects of job satisfaction and the likelihood that a worker votes for union representation. Up to 50 percent of the variance in employee voting behavior in these settings is explained by variations in job satisfaction.

Analyses of employee voting data also provide strong evidence of the importance of an economic calculus of the advantages of unionizing on a worker's choice. In one study of data from thirty-one union representation elections held during the early 1970s, the likelihood that a worker would vote for unionization was inversely related to his position in the wage distribution of the firm and to personal concerns over job security when alternative jobs were not easily available. Workers who expected unions to increase fairness of treatment and the likelihood of promotions also were more likely to vote union, as were black workers and younger workers.[11] Another indication of the importance of equity considerations

9. The objective of the instant election procedure, used in some provinces of Canada, is to eliminate the opportunities for unfair labor practices that a long campaign permits.

10. Herbert G. Heneman III and Marcus H. Sandver, "Predicting the Outcome of Union Certification Elections: A Review of the Literature," *Industrial and Labor Relations Review,* vol. 36 (July 1983), pp. 539–44.

11. Henry S. Farber and Daniel H. Saks, "Why Workers Want Unions: The Role of Relative Wages and Job Characteristics," *Journal of Political Economy,* vol. 88 (April 1980), pp. 349–69.

is that unions are more likely to win elections in industries in which the nonunion wage dispersions are relatively narrow.[12]

The important implication in all of this research is that workers are likely to enter a union representation campaign with a fairly strong predisposition to base their vote for a union or the employer on their knowledge of employment conditions and their expectations about how unions are likely to influence them. These studies of voting behavior in union elections, like the studies of union membership levels, find many factors other than campaign strategy and behavior that determine the pattern of union representation.

Yet worker job satisfaction and the perceived economic advantages of unionizing receive little or no attention in studies of workers' voting choice that use individual elections as their unit of analysis.[13] These studies relate election results to characteristics of the bargaining units and industries involved (on which data are readily available) rather than to workers' perceptions of the benefits of union representation. Interestingly, the most consistent result of these cross-section studies of individual elections is that union election success is inversely related to the number of workers in the election unit. But that result is at variance with the time series fact that both the proportion of union victories and unit size have declined over time. In 1950, election units averaged 159 workers and unions won 74 percent of representation elections. In 1980, election units averaged 66 employees and unions won 46 percent of the elections.[14] None of the studies has sought to explain this anomaly.

In general, the election-level studies reveal little about how workers would make their voting choice in the absence of illegal behavior. Some of the studies do attempt to address the influence of illegal behavior and regulation on election outcomes, however.[15] Here the distinction should

---

12. William T. Dickens, Douglas R. Wholey, and James C. Robinson, "Bargaining Unit, Union, Industry, and Locational Correlates of Union Support in Certification and Decertification Elections," NBER Working Paper 1671 (Cambridge, Mass.: National Bureau of Economic Research, July 1985).

13. Twenty-one of these studies are surveyed in Heneman and Sandver, "Predicting the Outcome," pp. 544–51.

14. A multiple regression analysis of state data over time finds that there is a 0.5 percentage point reduction in the proportion of workers voting for union representation for each ten-person reduction in election unit size; Ronald L. Seeber and William N. Cooke, "The Decline in Union Success in NLRB Representation Elections," *Industrial Relations*, vol. 22 (Winter 1983), pp. 34–44.

15. John Drotning, "NLRB Remedies for Election Misconduct: An Analysis of Election Outcomes and Their Determinants," *Journal of Business*, vol. 40 (April 1967), pp. 137–48; Richard Ulric Miller and George F. Leaming, "The Extent and Significance

be made between efforts to assess the impact of illegal activity (measured either directly or indirectly) and efforts to assess the effect of the time delays that can result from simply using the regulatory procedures established in the administration of the NLRA. The studies yield conflicting results regarding the effect of employers' unfair labor practices on election results. In a study of 368 representation elections, the General Accounting Office (GAO) found that the union success rate was higher in cases where there was no employer violation of the NLRA than in cases where there was a violation (45 percent versus 38 percent).[16] The GAO study, which focused on discriminatory discharges of union supporters, provides no indication of the statistical significance of the results. On the other hand, an AFL-CIO survey found that discharges for union activity had no impact on overall election success (although other types of unfair labor practice reduced the likelihood of winning an election in service industries).[17] A study of 760 elections involving a single national union in one NLRB region found no significant association between the commission of unfair labor practices and the percent of elections won by unions. Nor was there any significant difference in vote loss (the difference between the percent of workers signing authorization cards and the percent later voting for the union) in elections with and without unfair labor practices.[18]

---

of Administrative Delays in the Processing of Union Representation Cases in Arizona," *Arizona Review of Business and Public Administration,* vol. 11 (September 1962), pp. 1–11; Richard Prosten, "The Longest Season: Union Organizing in the Last Decade, a/k/a How Come One Team Has to Play with Its Shoelaces Tied Together?" and Myron Roomkin and Hervey A. Juris, "Unions in the Traditional Sectors: The Mid-Life Passage of the Labor Movement," in Barbara D. Dennis, ed., *Proceedings of the Thirty-First Annual Meeting of the Industrial Relations Research Association* (Madison, Wisc.: IRRA, 1979), pp. 240–49 and 212–22; Myron Roomkin and Richard N. Block, "Case Processing Time and the Outcome of Representation Elections: Some Empirical Evidence," *University of Illinois Law Review,* vol. 1981, no. 1 (1981), pp. 75–97; General Accounting Office, *Concerns Regarding Impact of Employee Charges against Employers for Unfair Labor Practices,* GAO/HRD–82–80 (GAO, 1982); William N. Cooke, "Determinants of the Outcomes of Union Certification Elections," *Industrial and Labor Relations Review,* vol. 36 (April 1983), pp. 402–14; Dickens, Wholey, and Robinson, "Bargaining Unit"; Laura Cooper, "Authorization Cards and Union Representation Election Outcome: An Empirical Assessment of the Assumption Underlying the Supreme Court's *Gissel* Decision," *Northwestern University Law Review,* vol. 79 (March 1984), pp. 87–141; AFL-CIO Department of Organization and Field Services, "AFL-CIO Organizing Survey" (Washington, April 1984).

16. GAO, *Concerns Regarding Impact of Employee Charges,* pp. 9–10.

17. "AFL-CIO Organizing Survey," pp. 7, 35. Interestingly, the use of management consultants in representation campaigns, a practice that many unions object to strongly, has no significant impact on election outcomes in this survey. Ibid., p. 36.

18. Cooper, "Authorization Cards," pp. 113–18.

A more consistent finding of these studies is that the percentage of union victories is inversely related to the length of time between filing a petition and holding an election. Is it the fact of delay or the specific illegal act (that culminates in delay-producing litigation) that reduces the likelihood of a union victory in representation elections? There has been no examination of this distinction in any of the studies of NLRB elections. It is clear, however, that employers could achieve procedural delays simply by filing many charges against unions. When the budgetary resources of a regulatory agency are limited, as are the NLRB's, each additional charge imposes a congestion cost on the entire regulatory system by lengthening the time that is required to decide each charge. Procedural maneuvers that delay the filing and conclusion of charges have been shown to have increased since the 1960s.[19] In response, unions could seek to reduce the period of adjudication by limiting the number of unfair labor practice charges filed. In the data gathered in one study, for example, slightly over half of the apparent violations of the act resulted in the filing of an unfair practice charge.[20] The effect of this incentive on employer compliance and union filing behavior is analyzed in chapter 5.

The studies at the election unit level suffer from serious defects in their efforts to ascertain the impact of the NLRA on election outcomes. They generally include no model of how workers would have made their union representation choice in the absence of a regulatory effect. The empirical tests are constructed as if the only factor determining voting behavior is regulatory delay or employer discrimination against union supporters. Only the GAO study was designed to ascertain the effects on voting of campaign conduct that is subject to NLRA regulation. And even that study relies on allegations of discriminatory acts rather than direct evidence of illegal behavior.

The first major attempt to deal with these shortcomings was Getman, Goldberg, and Herman's study of voting behavior and campaign conduct in thirty-one union representation elections in the Midwest and South

19. Surveys by the Industrial Union Department of the AFL-CIO indicate that in 1962, "11.3 percent of all NLRB elections were conducted in the same month as the original filing, and 59.2 percent of the elections had been concluded by the end of the month after the month of filing. The corresponding figures for 1977 were only 2.2 percent and 40 percent respectively." Richard Prosten, "Comment" on Rees, "Size of Union Membership," in Juris and Roomkin, *The Shrinking Perimeter,* p. 60.

20. Computed from data used in Julius G. Getman, Stephen B. Goldberg, and Jeanne B. Herman, *Union Representation Elections: Law and Reality* (New York: Russell Sage Foundation, 1976).

during the early 1970s.[21] Through interviews and questionnaires, the authors gathered information on the personal characteristics, job attitudes, voting intentions, and perceptions of the campaign by the employee-voters. And they kept a log of campaign conduct that they submitted to an experienced administrative law judge for the NLRB to obtain advisory rulings on the legality of the conduct.

The study analyzed the voting intentions of employees when the petition for an election was filed (before they were exposed to the main campaign) and the actual vote in the representation election. Attention focused on tactics during the campaign period that might have affected voting intentions. On the basis of the data gathered, the authors concluded that the initial voting intentions of employees are related to current job satisfaction and general philosophical attitudes toward unions. Indeed, with this information alone, they were able to predict the outcome of twenty-nine of the elections examined. Little that occurred during the campaign—including illegal discharge of some workers—had a significant effect in altering those intentions. The results of the study, which have stirred a great deal of controversy, suggest that the campaign activity that forms such a large proportion of the NLRB's unfair labor practice workload has little bearing on the basic right to an uncoerced choice for or against unionization that the Board's rules purportedly protect.[22]

The study indicates that the vote-switching that does occur tends to be from union to employer rather than the reverse. Union and company supporters among the employees are equally familiar with the company campaign (perhaps because they are a "captive audience" at meetings held on company time), but company supporters are much less familiar with the union campaign than are union supporters. (The authors suggest

21. Ibid. For a mixed commentary on the study, see "Symposium: Four Perspectives on *Union Representation Elections: Law and Reality,*" *Stanford Law Review,* vol. 28 (July 1976), pp. 1161–1205. For criticism of the study, see Paul Weiler, "Promises to Keep: Securing Workers' Rights to Self-Organization Under the NLRA," *Harvard Law Review,* vol. 96 (June 1983), pp. 1781–86. The authors respond to their critics in Stephen B. Goldberg, Julius G. Getman, and Jeanne M. Brett, "The Relationship Between Free Choice and Labor Board Doctrine: Differing Empirical Approaches," *Northwestern University Law Review,* vol. 79 (November 1984), pp. 721–35.

22. Doubts concerning the impact of NLRB regulation on employee voting behavior had been expressed much earlier in Derek C. Bok, "The Regulation of Campaign Tactics in Representation Elections Under the National Labor Relations Act," *Harvard Law Review,* vol. 78 (November 1964), pp. 38–141.

that unions should get more access to employees during a representation campaign.)

According to the study, the basic behavioral assumptions underlying the NLRB's regulation are not valid. While the Board attempts to replicate laboratory campaign conditions, the majority of employees are inattentive to the campaign. Many have worked for unionized firms and already know about unions and industrial relations. Campaign information is subject to perceptual distortion—employees who are pro-union are likely to interpret an employer's speech as more threatening than workers who support the employer but to accept it as further evidence of the need for union representation. The general picture that emerges from the study is that misinformation, threatening behavior, and promises of benefit do not affect workers in ways that are likely to have a coercive influence on the choice of a union.

In concluding that most of the election campaign behavior regulated by the NLRB does not interfere with workers' free choice of union representative, the Getman study provides one strain of academic researchers' case for deregulation.[23] The study has been criticized for its rather limited use of multivariate statistical methods despite the fact that there are likely to be several simultaneous influences on the voting choices being made. The authors often interpret results that fall below conventional standards of statistical significance as having no substantive impact on the phenomenon (voting behavior) under study (rather than acknowledging that there is an effect that is imprecisely measured). And critics argue that because many union representation elections are decided by a very small margin of votes, even a small effect of illegal campaign activity can change an election result. Given the behavior patterns of both unions and management in campaigns for union representation, the results of the study also appear to contrast sharply with strongly held beliefs on both sides.

Some of the criticisms have been addressed in a substantial reanalysis of the Getman data by William Dickens.[24] Dickens's model relates the probability that a worker votes for a union to thirty variables constructed from the Getman data. The variables that pertain to individual back-

---

23. Another strain, noted in chapter 1, comes from an opposition to institutions that reduce competition in labor markets.

24. William T. Dickens, "The Effect of Company Campaigns on Certification Elections: *Law and Reality* Once Again," *Industrial and Labor Relations Review*, vol. 36 (July 1983), pp. 560–75.

ground include the initial voting disposition of workers, their expectation of the potential wage changes associated with unionization, and a number of demographic characteristics. Those that pertain to the election background mainly identify the individual unions involved, while the remaining variables measure legal and illegal campaign activities, including speeches, actions, and types of employer and worker contacts during the campaign period.

The reanalysis confirms that the dominant influence on voting behavior in union representation elections is workers' initial predispositions (which appear to depend on job satisfaction and philosophical attitudes toward unions). Thus, much of the voting pattern observed in the elections appears to be determined long before the beginning of the campaigns that the NLRB regulates.

Like the Getman study, Dickens finds that neither illegal speech nor general illegal actions has a statistically significant relation to the likelihood that a worker will vote for union representation.[25] The average effect of such actions is to reduce the probability of voting union by 2 percentage points, with the 95 percent confidence interval ranging from a 10 percent increase in the probability of voting union if workers feel they need the protection of a union to a 15 percent reduction if they do not.

Unlike the Getman study, however, Dickens finds that threats and actions against employees identified as union supporters are associated with a statistically significant average reduction in the probability of voting union of 15.5 percent. He also produces simulation evidence indicating that even small effects on the probability of voting union can have a notable tendency to change election outcomes. For example, if each employee's probability of voting union increased by 1 percent, there would be a 2 percent increase in the proportion of elections won by unions. If the probability increased by 5 percent, the percentage won would increase by 9 percent.[26]

DETERMINANTS OF ELECTION OUTCOMES. Although the studies of election outcomes are methodologically diverse, they reveal a few central ten-

25. Dickens defines illegal speech as "any general promises of benefits or threats of retaliation directed at all workers, or any statement judged to be misleading," and illegal actions as "any benefit granted to all workers; retaliation made against all workers; interrogation of employees or surveillance of employees' union activities; failure to hire pro-union workers; or dealing with an employee committee before the election." Ibid., p. 566.

26. Ibid., p. 572.

dencies. While representation elections are the main channel of regulatory influence on unionization, election outcomes are not the only, or in some periods even the main, determinant of union membership. The principal factors that influence a worker's union representation choice are long-term predispositions related to job and income satisfaction. Once noncampaign factors in union elections are controlled for, considerable uncertainty surrounds the impact of specific unfair labor practices established in the NLRA; it appears, however, that much campaign speech the NLRB finds illegal has no practical effect on election outcomes. There is wide agreement that delays in holding elections, whether due to procedural maneuvers or to congestion in the adjudication system, reduce the probability that a union will win an election.

Negotiation of Labor Agreements

Victory in a representation election confers on a union the status of exclusive representative of the workers in the bargaining unit. But this right means little until a contract is negotiated, and even a contract means little if it fails to improve employment conditions. It therefore comes as a surprise to many observers to learn that the regulation established by the NLRA is directed at labor relations procedures rather than outcomes. In principle, the statute does not seek to achieve a particular result or even to equalize bargaining power between labor and management.

The tension between a procedural and a substantive orientation is evident in the congressional debate that preceded establishment of a policy toward unions. In passing the NLRA, Congress apparently wished to keep the government regulatory apparatus outside the substance of collective bargaining. Few people in or out of Congress felt that the right to organize would have value if a contract was not signed, however. Hence the duty to bargain in good faith that was imposed on employers (in section 8.a.5) in 1935 and on unions (in section 8.b.3) in 1947.

The good-faith provision has been controversial since the earliest days of the NLRA. In terms of the impact of the law, it raises a procedural question. Is its objective to assist in the establishment of a contractual relationship between a union and employer? More problematically, does the presence of a duty to bargain alter contract outcomes?

Many union election victories are not followed by labor agreements.

In the 1970s, for example, no contract was negotiated in about a quarter of the bargaining units in which a majority of the employees voted for union representation.[27] Few studies have been made of the factors that influence the probability that a union winning a representation election will negotiate an initial collective bargaining agreement. One study of a nationwide sample of newly organized units indicated that the existence of other labor agreements in a firm and the presence of a national union representative in negotiations both raised the likelihood that an agreement would be signed. But the likelihood of completing an initial agreement fell as the number of unfair labor practice charges filed during negotiations grew.[28]

In a related study of 118 efforts at initial contract negotiations in Indiana following union election victories in 1979 and 1980, 77 percent of the units won a contract—about the same as in the nationwide sample. One way that employers can postpone initial negotiations is by filing objections to the election conduct and refusing to bargain until their objections are resolved. The Indiana study found that the likelihood of negotiating an agreement declined as the delay involved in resolving objections grew longer. It also found that discharges of one or more union supporters cut the likelihood of a first agreement almost in half. There is no way of knowing whether it is the discharge itself or the fact that it is not remedied immediately that affects the outcome. And discharges probably tend to occur where unions are weak anyway and therefore would have difficulty in establishing an initial agreement.[29]

More surprisingly (and less certain statistically), the results seemed to indicate that allegations of failure to bargain in good faith also reduced the likelihood that a contract would be negotiated. Interpreted literally, the statutory provision intended to increase the likelihood that a contract would be signed appears to have the opposite effect. Although the effect is imprecisely measured (the t-statistic is -1.52), the Indiana estimate implies that filing a duty-to-bargain charge reduces the likelihood of winning an initial contract by 25 percent.[30]

27. Prosten, "The Longest Season"; William N. Cooke, *Union Organizing and Public Policy: Failure to Secure First Contracts* (Kalamazoo, Mich.: W. E. Upjohn Institute for Employment Research, 1985).

28. Cooke, *Union Organizing*, chap 3.

29. William N. Cooke, "The Failure to Negotiate First Contracts: Determinants and Policy Implications," *Industrial and Labor Relations Review*, vol. 38 (January 1985), pp. 163–78, and *Union Organizing*, chap. 3.

30. Cooke, "Failure to Negotiate First Contracts," pp. 174–75.

Accepting this result at face value ignores the realities of an effort to negotiate a first agreement. If the NLRA did not exist, the outcome would depend on the relative bargaining strengths of the two parties. When an employer perceives that the cost of resisting a union's demand for a contract exceeds the cost of operating under the terms of an agreement—when the union has the power to impose high costs—a contract will be signed. The quality of the contract will also depend on the extent to which the union can impose costs on a recalcitrant employer.

Under the NLRA, unions that have enough power to obtain an initial contract without invoking a duty to bargain are unlikely to have to resort to the unfair labor practice procedures. And those that are unlikely to obtain a contract in the absence of legislation will probably have to use statutory procedures in an effort to improve their weak position. The Indiana results may simply be revealing that unions that are least likely to obtain a contract through normal collective bargaining resort to the unfair labor practice procedures. Filing an unfair labor practice charge may signal an inherent weakness in bargaining power. If only the weakest unions use the statute, the statistical result may indicate more about the choice of methods than the marginal effect of the law. Unfortunately, there are no studies of the impact of the NLRA on the likelihood of obtaining a first contract that control for selection bias. Since the statutory duty to bargain does not compel the parties to reach agreement or even to make concessions, it seems unlikely that it raises the odds of obtaining a contract for weak unions.[31]

Once a collective bargaining agreement is established, there is the further question of the influence of the legal obligation to bargain on the scope and contents of the agreement. NLRB policy permits bargaining of mandatory issues to impasse and work stoppage but finds insistence on bargaining a voluntary issue to the point of impasse by either party a violation of the duty to bargain in good faith.[32]

31. In 1958 an appeals court decision posed this question: "Can the company's insistence on terms overall favorable to it in net result be taken as proof that it did not approach the bargaining table in good faith, but that it approached the bargaining table only to give the outward sign of compliance when it had already excluded the possibility of agreement?" A majority of the court answered no and set aside an NLRB finding that this constituted an illegal refusal to bargain. *White* v. *NLRB,* 225 F.2d 564, 566 (5th Cir. 1958).

32. *Wooster Division of Borg-Warner Corp.,* 113 N.L.R.B. 1288 (1955), *aff'd,* 356 U.S. 342 (1958). The finding is based on the overriding purpose of the NLRA to reduce industrial unrest that is not necessary to attain its objectives.

In the process of classifying issues as mandatory or voluntary, the Board effectively determines legal reinstatement rights and thereby influences the likelihood that a contract demand can be backed by the use of force. Resistance to a demand considered to be mandatory is more costly than resistance to the same demand found to be voluntary. By altering the cost of resistance, rulings by the NLRB can alter the relative bargaining power of unions and management. Topics labeled mandatory are more likely to end up in collective-bargaining agreements than topics labeled voluntary simply because the ability to use force to back up mandatory demands raises the probability that they will be accepted. On very narrow issues, then, NLRB rulings could alter the substance of the collective bargaining agreement when the contract is viewed on an issue-by-issue basis, but their influence over a spectrum of issues is less certain. If several issues are under negotiation, either party may be able to bring force to bear in support of a voluntary issue simply by letting an impasse develop over a mandatory issue that can only be settled after the voluntary issue is resolved. To date there have been no empirical studies of this question.

Overall Union Representation

Contemporary evaluations of labor policy in the United States often conclude that union growth has been retarded by employers' increasing resort to unfair labor practices.[33] The sharp increase in remedial awards for illegal discharges in the late 1970s and the steep decline in the proportion of representation elections won by unions—down from 75 percent in the early 1950s to about 45 percent thirty years later—are frequently cited to support this conclusion.[34] However, the fact of declining union representation is clearer than is the effect of the decline on union power during the 1970s, for the difference between union and nonunion wages increased substantially in that decade. For some workers, at least, the returns from union membership were increasing at a time when the representation statistics suggest that unions were becoming less powerful.

33. Paul Weiler, "Promises to Keep," and "Striking a New Balance: Freedom of Contract and the Prospects for Union Representation," *Harvard Law Review*, vol. 98 (December 1984), pp. 351–420; AFL-CIO, *The Changing Situation*.
34. Data are from *Annual Report of the National Labor Relations Board*, various years.

In contrast to the policy discussions and legal analyses of union representation, most economic analyses of union membership have accorded no attention to the role of unfair labor practices or national labor relations policy generally.[35] The economic studies generally make the explicit assumption that workers balance the benefits and costs of union and nonunion employment and choose the alternative that offers the highest net benefit. By according a passive role to the employer, these studies are structured as if practices forbidden by the NLRA have no bearing on the benefits or costs of union representation.[36] Empirically, the economic studies stress the influence of differences in the levels of union and nonunion compensation on union representation, a factor ignored in most studies of the relation between illegal labor relations behavior and unionization.

Clearly, neither of these approaches separates the effects of behavior addressed by the NLRA from more general economic changes on union representation. In addition, the traditional economic analyses, if taken at face value, present a puzzle for interpreting developments during the 1970s. Between 1969 and 1982, a period in which unfair labor practice charges doubled, the ratio of union to nonunion wages rose steadily.[37] Cross-section economic studies of the determinants of union membership suggest that the growth in the relative attractiveness of union employment should have increased representation. What explains the fact that it did not?

Representation, Relative Wages, and Unfair Practices

If the influences of economic and NLRA-related factors are to be disentangled, simple tabulations of data are not sufficient. What is needed

35. Henry S. Farber and Daniel H. Saks, "Why Workers Want Unions: The Role of Relative Wages and Job Characteristics," *Journal of Political Economy*, vol. 88 (April 1980), pp. 349–69; Lung-Fei Lee, "Unionism and Wage Rates: A Simultaneous Equations Model With Qualitative and Limited Dependent Variables," *International Economic Review*, vol. 19 (June 1978), pp. 415–33.

36. Implicitly, these studies adopt the controversial conclusion reached in Getman, Goldberg, and Herman, *Union Representation Elections*.

37. Robert J. Flanagan, "Wage Concessions and Long-Term Union Wage Flexibility," *Brookings Papers on Economic Activity, 1:1984*, pp. 186–88; George E. Johnson, "Changes Over Time in the Union-Nonunion Wage Differential in the United States," in Jean-Jacques Rosa, ed., *The Economics of Trade Unions: New Directions* (Boston: Kluwer-Nijhoff, 1984), pp. 5–7. The growth of the union relative wage during the 1970s provides a caution against casual empiricism when dealing with complicated social phenomena. Few observers seem to conclude that the increase in regulatory litigation caused the union relative wage to rise.

instead is an explicit model of the main behavioral relationships, implemented by statistical estimation techniques that correct for the interactions between different parts of the model.

Economywide union representation reflects the interplay of worker and employer choices. Workers presumably balance the benefits and costs of union representation in making the job choices or voting decisions that determine their union status. The most plausible hypothesis is simply that the proportion of the labor force interested in union representation increases as the relative advantage of union over nonunion wages increases.[38] The higher the union relative wage, the more attractive it is and the more likely to compensate for the higher probability of unemployment in union jobs and for any other reservations that workers may have about union representation. For groups such as women and nonwhites, whose earnings in the nonunion sector are relatively low, the going union rate may be particularly attractive. Worker interest in union representation therefore should increase with each group's representation in the labor force.

Whether or not employers' unfair labor practices influence the supply of workers interested in unionizing is a matter of controversy reviewed earlier. To the extent that employer behavior does have a coercive effect, the supply of workers interested in unionizing will shift upward (to the left). That is, it will take a larger union-nonunion wage differential to induce union support in the face of illegal employer resistance. Alternatively, to the extent that illegal employer behavior convinces workers that they must take collective action to counter employer power, the supply function will shift downward (to the right). A lower union relative wage will induce a given fraction of the labor force to join a union. Parallel arguments may be advanced concerning increasing unfair labor practice charges filed by individual workers against unions. The greater the doubts about the quality of union representation, the more unions will have to demonstrate they can offer in order to induce support. In equation form, worker interest in union representation in year t is:

$$(1) \qquad U_t^s = a_0 + a_1\, RELWAGE_t + a_2\, NONWHITE_t$$
$$+ a_3\, FEMALE_t + a_4\, ULP_t + e_t,$$
$$a_1, a_2, a_3 > 0, a_4 \gtrless 0$$

in which U^s is the proportion of the labor force interested in union

---

38. Farber and Saks, "Why Workers Want Unions"; Lee, "Unionism and Wage Rates."

representation, *RELWAGE* the union-nonunion wage differential,[39] *NONWHITE* and *FEMALE* the labor force fractions of each group, *ULP* the number of unfair labor practice charges, and *e* the error. The inequalities indicate that increases in relative wages, the percent of nonwhites, and the percent of females are expected to increase the proportion of the work force interested in union representation, and an increase in unfair labor practice charges is expected to decrease the proportion interested in representation.

The employers' side of the market is equally straightforward. Profit-maximizing employers have an incentive to substitute toward relatively inexpensive production methods, and utility-maximizing consumers have an incentive to substitute toward relatively inexpensive products. Increases in the difference between union and nonunion wages induce employers and consumers to search for cheaper production methods and products and tend to reduce the fraction of employment that is unionized. On their side of the market, the relation between the union relative wage and the ratio of union to nonunion employment is negative. The entire relationship will be affected by economic growth and recession. In equation form, the employer's relative demand for union labor in year *t* is:

$$(2) \qquad U_t^d = b_0 + b_1 \, RELWAGE_t + b_2 \, EMPCHG_t + e_t,$$
$$b_1 < 0$$

in which *EMPCHG* is the rate of change of nonagricultural employment. The inequality indicates that increases in the union relative wage are expected to decrease the relative demand by employers for union workers.

The relationships between the union relative wage and the extent of unionization on both the employers' and the workers' sides can be considered along with the role of unfair labor practice charges, which themselves reflect the influence of the union relative wage through its effect on compliance and enforcement incentives. The results of a two-stage least-squares analysis of these relationships are reported in table 4-1. They confirm the basic hypotheses that the desire of workers for unionization increases as the difference between union and nonunion wages increases (regression 1) and that employers' relative demand for union workers declines as the union relative wage increases (regression 3). The effect on the demand for labor is over three times stronger than the effect on the supply.

39. In the empirical work, the log of the relative wage is used.

Table 4-1. Regressions of a Model of Union Representation

Variable[a]	Regression 1[b]	Regression 2[b]	Regression 3[b]
Constant term	60.58	62.14	31.14
	(3.04)	(3.29)	(27.87)
Wage differential, *RELWAGE*	0.25	0.25	−0.89
	(2.01)	(1.98)	(2.80)
Nonwhite fraction of			
labor force, *NONWHITE*	−3.02	−2.57	...
	(2.06)	(1.60)	
Female fraction of			
labor force, *FEMALE*	0.12	−0.08	...
	(0.24)	(0.21)	
Unfair labor practice			
charges, *ULP*	−0.00023	...	...
	(1.24)		
Unfair labor practice charges			
against employers, *EMPULP*	...	−0.00027	...
		(1.25)	
Rate of change of nonagricultural			
unemployment, *EMPCHG*	...	...	−0.37
			(1.11)
Standard error of estimate	0.936	0.958	4.21

Sources: National Labor Relations Board, Office of Statistical Services; George E. Johnson, "Changes Over Time in the Union-Nonunion Wage Differential in the United States," in Jean-Jacques Rosa, ed., *The Economics of Trade Unions: New Directions* (Boston: Kluwer-Nijhoff, 1984), pp. 5–7; *Employment and Training Report of the President, 1982* (Government Printing Office, 1983).

a. Variables defined in the text.

b. Results are from a two-stage least-squares regression. Numbers in parentheses are *t*-statistics.

In addition to the direct influence of the union relative wage on the demand for union members, there is a potential indirect effect through its influence on employers' decisions to comply with the NLRA. The general effect of an increase in the difference between union and nonunion compensation provides incentives for employers to reduce their compliance with the statute and for unions and workers to challenge potential noncompliance by filing unfair labor practice charges. This potential effect is not realized, however, because the relationship between charges of unfair labor practices and union representation, while negative, is measured so imprecisely that it falls well below normal standards of statistical significance (regression 1).

The charges included in the variable in regression 1 are those filed by all parties. Because much of the controversy concerning the effect of the NLRA on representation is directed at employer behavior, only the unfair labor practice charges filed against employers are represented in regression 2. The narrower definition of charges produces no increase in statistical significance. And regressions using charges by individual workers against unions as a measure of unfair labor practice produce even less precise results than those reported in table 4-1, casting doubt on the hypothesis that declining fortunes of unions reflect worker disaffection with the quality of representation.

In short, the aggregate data do not provide strong support for a connection between unfair labor practice charges and union representation. Instead, the direct effect of the growing relative expense of union labor appears to be the more powerful influence on declining representation.

Regulation, Labor Relations, and Unionization

Much of the evidence on what determines the outcome of union elections points to the importance of nonregulatory factors in shaping voting behavior. Clearly, employers who may wish to avoid unions have options other than violating the NLRA. Indeed, the evidence implies that the response to policy changes that increase the cost of violating the NLRA is likely to be changes in human resource management techniques aimed at increasing workers' job satisfaction. Therefore, unions are unlikely to be able to regain all of the ground they believe they have lost because of the weak remedies and slack administration of the act.

Studies of the impact of NLRB regulation on labor relations outcomes provide little guidance on how regulatory rules might be changed. When full account is taken of the methodological issues raised by such studies, it is tempting to suggest that the strength of the estimated impact is inversely related to the quality of the study. In particular, the more careful the specification of worker job attitudes and predispositions to vote union, the weaker is the estimated impact of illegal behavior. Some of the policy variables that appear to influence outcomes in the more careful studies are related to broad categories of activity rather than the specific legal categories of violation that the NLRB rules on. For example, studies of the effects of delays fail to distinguish delays in general from specific violations that give rise to delays. The impact of certain kinds of violations—union unfair labor practice charges in particular—has yet to be studied.

The evidence, however tenuous, nonetheless indicates that at least some violations of the NLRA by employers can alter labor relations outcomes in a way that is favorable to employers, thereby creating an incentive for noncompliance. The puzzle of why this incentive should have changed over time to produce the growing gap between unfair labor practices and labor relations activity is addressed analytically in chapter 5.

The discovery of some links between noncompliance and labor relations outcomes at the micro level is not equivalent to establishing a significant link between noncompliance and overall union representation at the macro level. There are many factors beyond the domain of the NLRA that have an influence on the proportion of workers who are unionized. The analysis in this chapter indicates that market adjustments to the rise in the union relative wage have had a more profound effect on union coverage of the work force than the growth of unfair labor practice charges. Thus structural reforms in regulatory procedures—for example, shifting to the system of instant elections used in some Canadian provinces—would probably have a limited effect on aggregate union representation. They could, however, produce real savings in resource costs by reducing the litigiousness that NLRB procedures currently promote. The results of the regressions described in this chapter cast doubt on the possibility that changes in labor policy can have a broad influence on the degree of union representation.

CHAPTER 5

Compliance with the NLRA

NEITHER CHANGES in the volume of regulated labor relations nor general changes in the economic environment explain the growth in regulatory litigation under the National Labor Relations Act. Nor do changes in the distribution of these activities by industry or region. Much of the growth of regulatory activity must therefore reflect the response of the parties to collective bargaining to their environment and to the incentives established by the statute itself.

At the core of this behavioral response are decisions to comply with and to monitor and enforce compliance with the NLRA. Some observers argue that an important reason for both the surge in regulatory litigation and the decline in union representation has been the growing failure of employers to comply with the NLRA. This chapter explores the relation between compliance decisions and incentives to comply and compares American employers' resistance to unions and collective bargaining with the actions of their European counterparts.

The Compliance Process

Strategic play under the NLRA begins when one party (say, the employer) in a union organizing campaign or collective bargaining negotiations decides on a course of action. The other party (a union or a worker) then decides whether to challenge the behavior by filing an unfair labor practice charge. As with civil torts, antitrust suits, and other legal actions in which the potential violation and the perpetrator are easily identified, enforcement is initiated by a victim, the party to the

73

employment relationship or collective bargaining agreement who files an unfair labor practice charge.[1]

A third party, the National Labor Relations Board, investigates charges and decides the case. The stages in the NLRB procedure have been described by a former general counsel of the Board:

> The Agency does not have complete control over its case intake, and it must respond to all inquiries concerning possible violations of the National Labor Relations Act. . . . [A] newly filed charge is investigated first for merit and, if found to be meritorious, the parties are encouraged to settle without further action. Non-meritorious cases are withdrawn or dismissed. If a case is found to have merit and no initial settlement is reached, then a complaint is issued and a hearing held before an Administrative Law Judge. Following the hearing and the Judge's decision, there may be further appeals to the Board and the Courts of Appeal. At any point in the process, the parties may reach a settlement agreed to by the Agency, alleviating the need for further proceedings.[2]

Like the courts but unlike some regulatory or compliance agencies, the NLRB cannot choose which cases to audit. It must consider all charges brought by unions, employers, and individual workers. Moreover, by assuming the burden of investigation, the Board substantially reduces for plaintiffs the cost of filing a charge.

Several aspects of this process are notable. First, the victim has a definite choice to make concerning the initiation of enforcement proceedings, and there is evidence that much illegal behavior goes unreported.[3] On the other hand, many allegations of unfair labor practice are found to be without merit. In recent years, about 35 percent of the charges filed have been dismissed or withdrawn after investigation and

---

1. If a union or employer fails to challenge behavior that constitutes a potential violation of the NLRA, any employee may file an unfair labor practice charge. Thus victims may introduce an element of competition into the process that results in optimal enforcement of the law. See Gary S. Becker and George J. Stigler, "Law Enforcement, Malfeasance, and Compensation of Enforcers," and William M. Landes and Richard A. Posner, "The Private Enforcement of Law," *Journal of Legal Studies,* vol. 3 (January 1974), pp. 1–18, and vol. 4 (January 1975), pp. 1–46.

2. Testimony of William A. Lubbers, in *Departments of Labor, Health and Human Services, Education, and Related Agencies Appropriations for 1985,* Hearings before the Subcommittee on the Departments of Labor, Health and Human Services, Education, and Related Agencies of the House Committee on Appropriations, 98 Cong. 2 sess. (GPO, 1984), pt. 7: *Related Agencies,* pp. 561–62.

3. Julius G. Getman, Stephen B. Goldberg, and Jeanne B. Herman, *Union Representation Elections: Law and Reality* (New York: Russell Sage Foundation, 1976), found charges filed in only 53 percent of the cases in which an administrative law judge found the behavior in violation of the law.

discussion by the regional offices of the Board.[4] Only a small proportion of the meritorious charges ever reaches formal adjudication by an administrative law judge or the Board—a feature that this compliance process shares with the U.S. court system generally.[5]

The decisions of each party in the process depend in part on the actions it expects the other party and the NLRB to take. For example, an employer's choice of behavior will depend on the likelihood of inducing an unfair labor practice charge and of the charge being successful. The choices are made in an environment of uncertainty over how the other party will respond and, in many areas of the law, how the NLRB will rule.

Remarkably little is known empirically about either the extent of compliance or changes in the level of compliance with the NLRA over its fifty-year history. The unfair labor practice charges that are observed are the joint outcome of decisions to comply with the law and decisions to press for enforcement. Therefore, an increase in the volume of regulatory litigation relative to labor relations activity may reflect increased noncompliance or increased incentives to enforce infractions of the act.

The difficulty of observing compliance directly is illustrated by considering several purported measures of compliance with the NLRA reported in table 5-1. On their face, they appear to indicate a decline in compliance under the act. Consider the most frequently cited evidence of noncompliance—the flow of unfair labor practice charges. Although suggestive, even these data do not offer precise evidence on trends in compliance, because the appearance of an unfair labor practice charge is the joint result of a choice of labor relations behavior and a choice to file an unfair labor practice charge. Variations in the likelihood that a particular labor relations practice will be challenged by the filing of a charge can occur independently of changes in compliance.

And the same ambiguity applies to the interpretation of the data indicating a sharp increase in the numbers of employees found to have been illegally discharged and awarded back pay for illegal employer actions. While the data are consistent with an increase in the general

4. National Labor Relations Board, Office of Statistical Services.

5. William M. Landes, "An Economic Analysis of the Courts," *Journal of Law and Economics,* vol. 14 (April 1971), pp. 61–107; George L. Priest and Benjamin Klein, "The Selection of Disputes for Litigation," *Journal of Legal Studies,* vol. 13 (January 1984), pp. 1–55.

Table 5-1. Indicators of Compliance with the NLRA, 1948, 1970, and 1980

Indicator	1948	1970	1980
Number of unfair labor practice cases filed	3,598	21,038	44,063
Number of workers offered reinstatement	1,001	3,779	10,033
As a percent of eligible voters	0.3	0.6	1.9
Number of workers receiving back pay	1,196	6,833	15,642
As a percent of eligible voters	0.3	1.1	3.0
Number of representation elections	3,319	8,074	8,240[a]
Number of consent elections	2,190	2,146	642[a]
Consent elections as a percent of total	66	27	8
Number of cases in which picketing ended	n.a.	676	753
Number of cases in which work stoppage ended	n.a.	349	198

Source: National Labor Relations Board, Office of Statistical Services.
n.a. Not available.
a. Data for 1978.

level of noncompliance, they could also reflect an increased tendency to use legal action to challenge employer behavior as collective bargaining or other devices for moderating employer behavior become less effective. Thus, an understanding of compliance requires knowing how compliance decisions and monitoring decisions are reached.

Evidence of a steep decline in consent elections is more clearly consistent with an increase in noncompliance by employers. In the early days of the NLRA, virtually all union representation elections were consent elections, agreed to by both the union and the employer. In 1950 consent elections constituted 66 percent of all elections, by 1980 only 8 percent. Over those years, stipulated elections rose from 10 percent to 76 percent of union representation elections.[6] By this measure, there has been a clear increase in employer resistance to attempts to form unions.

Why has compliance declined? If employers find it in their self-interest to violate the NLRA now, why was it not in their self-interest in the early 1950s? To what extent has the NLRB influenced the decrease in compliance and the increase in regulatory litigation reported in chapter 3? In what ways can it expect to influence these trends in the future? These questions can only be answered in the context of a deeper analysis of compliance and enforcement decisions under the NLRA.

6. Data from NLRB, Office of Statistical Services. See Richard Prosten, "The Longest Season: Union Organizing in the Last Decade, a/k/a How Come One Team Has to Play with Its Shoelaces Tied Together?" in Barbara D. Dennis, ed., *Proceedings of the Thirty-First Annual Meeting of the Industrial Relations Research Association* (Madison, Wisc.: IRRA, 1978), pp. 240–49.

The Compliance Game

The compliance process under the NLRA involves an interesting game between two parties with adversarial interests—unions and employers—and a regulatory agency, the National Labor Relations Board. (In an increasing number of instances a worker is a player, substituting for either the union or the employer in filing a charge.) Some labor relations activities are unquestionably legal under the existing doctrine of the NLRB and the federal courts. Some are clearly illegal. Both parties may be uncertain, however, about the legality of activities that do not exactly match activities in previous cases that have given rise to NLRB or court precedents. Or the precedents may be uncertain because the Board has reversed itself or issued inconsistent rulings. Or the Board may not have ruled on a similar set of facts (for example, on novel issues that may or may not be mandatory topics of bargaining, or employer speeches that walk a thin line between a threat and a prophecy of a plant closing if a union wins a representation campaign).

There appear to be many instances in which employers and unions comply voluntarily with the NLRA, no matter what the economic consequences. In an industrial relations system in which an average of 32,000 charges of unfair labor practices arose out of some 70,000 collective bargaining negotiations, 8,000 representation elections, and 5,000 work stoppages in a typical year in the 1970s, it appears likely that many employers and unions forgo opportunities to violate the NLRA.[7]

At times, one side may adopt a strategic stance toward the labor relations laws, letting its desire to maximize expected profits or wage payments govern the choice between safe behavior and uncertain or illegal behavior. In recent years, representatives of organized labor have argued that employers' behavior toward the NLRA is increasingly strategic.[8]

The key feature of a strategic approach to the law is that compliance

7. Figures based on data from NLRB, Office of Statistical Services; Bureau of Labor Statistics, *Analysis of Work Stoppages, 1979*, bulletin 2092 (Government Printing Office, 1981), p. 7. The number of charges reflects in part the unions' inclination to challenge employer behavior by filing unfair labor practice charges.

8. See *Oversight Hearings on the Subject "Has Labor Law Failed,"* Joint Hearings before the Subcommittee on Labor-Management Relations of the House Committee on Education and Labor and the Manpower and Housing Subcommittee of the House Committee on Government Operations, 98 Cong. 2 sess. (GPO, 1984), 2 vols.

incentives rather than ideological predispositions determine the choice of whether to obey the law or to resist unions. Under a strategic approach, compliance depends on a purely economic calculation by the employer and hence is determined by the structure of incentives under the regulatory framework of the NLRA. Differences among employers in their strategic behavior therefore reflect differences in the expected economic benefits and costs rather than in their ideological orientation toward unions. Acting strategically does not rule out compliance with the NLRA, if compliance will maximize expected profits.[9]

Similarly, unions base their decisions to challenge the behavior of employers on an economic analysis of the benefits and costs of filing an unfair labor practice charge. This does not rule out filing charges, but it does mean that under some circumstances a union may be better off by not filing a charge.

More generally, there may be strong economic reasons for behavior that is purportedly ideological. Ideologically based explanations of changes in compliance must first explain why a shift in the stance of employers toward unions has occurred.

Employer Compliance Decisions

How does a strategic employer decide what labor relations behavior to adopt, and how does a union decide whether to file an unfair practice charge? (In an average year, 70–75 percent of charges filed are against employers.) Each party begins with knowledge of the payoffs available from various kinds of behavior. A strategic, profit-maximizing employer is induced to consider activities of uncertain legality because, if unchallenged, they promise lower labor costs than activities that are clearly legal.[10] In some cases the influence on costs may be direct, as in probable violations of the duty to bargain. In others, such as probable violations

9. This is the same kind of approach that is described in Gary S. Becker, "Crime and Punishment: An Economic Approach," *Journal of Political Economy*, vol. 76 (March–April 1968), pp. 169–217; Jennifer F. Reinganum and Louis L. Wilde, "An Equilibrium Model of Tax Compliance with a Bayesian Auditor and Some 'Honest' Taxpayers," Social Science Working Paper 506 (California Institute of Technology, Division of Humanities and Social Sciences, December 1983).

10. These are not innocuous assumptions, for there is considerable controversy (reviewed in chap. 4) surrounding the actual impact of NLRB rule making on labor relations outcomes.

of the standards that govern employer behavior in union representation campaigns, costs may be indirectly affected, depending on the extent to which the probability of representation is reduced.

The payoff to an employer, in lower costs, from adopting behavior of uncertain legality increases with the expected impact of the union on compensation and with the size of the bargaining unit (if the presence of a union produces a wage premium). The payoff decreases as the size of the penalty for violating the labor relations laws increases, if there is a significant probability of detection. (For a formal description of the incentives facing a strategic employer, see the appendix.)

Detection depends on union or worker action. An employer's inducement to violate the law is tempered by the possibilities that a union or worker will challenge the behavior by filing an unfair labor practice charge and that the NLRB (and the federal courts, in an appeal) will sustain the charge. If a charge is filed, the employer incurs litigation costs no matter how the Board rules on the charge, and these costs must be balanced against the advantages of adopting the action giving rise to the charge. If the charge is sustained by the Board, the employer must in principle also pay the costs that would have been incurred if he had adopted legal behavior. Fines are unlikely since the NLRB is authorized only to impose remedies that restore the status quo as of the time that the violation occurred.

Clearly a central issue in the compliance game concerns how each party's expectations of success are formed. These expectations may simply be determined from the record of Board behavior, or they may be forward-looking, based on forecasts, for example, of how changes in the political composition of the Board will affect its decisions.

When the variety of benefits and costs is considered, an employer is more likely to choose borderline behavior the larger the bargaining unit, the larger the labor cost differential associated with illegal behavior, the lower the fine or the costs of litigation, the lower the probability that the union will file a charge, and the lower the probability of an adverse decision from the NLRB. Under the NLRA, both union (or worker) and NLRB actions influence an employer's expected costs and hence his choice of labor relations behavior.

When a union observes the employer's labor relations behavior, it realizes on the basis of past NLRB rulings that there is some probability that the behavior is in violation of the NLRA. When the legal status of an employer's action seems uncertain, the union must decide whether or not to file an unfair labor practice charge. If no charge is filed, union status or the compensation of union members is lower than it would have been if the employer had adopted safe labor relations behavior. By filing a charge, the union incurs litigation costs, but if a favorable Board ruling is obtained, the union's status and impact will theoretically be restored to the level at the time of the violation.[11] Since the normal legal fees of litigation for the filing party are borne by the General Counsel's Office of the NLRB, the cost to the union is in the opportunity costs of the time of union officials substantiating the charges and the delays in adjudication that arise from adding another charge to the system.

If punitive damages were permitted under the NLRA and were paid to plaintiffs whose charges prevailed, the expected return for filing a charge would be raised. If damages were paid into the U.S. Treasury, there would be no change in the union's incentive to file a charge. If the Board ruling is unfavorable, there is no return to be balanced against the litigation costs. Given the structure of incentives, a union will be more likely to file a charge the greater is the effect of the employer's behavior on the wage advantage of union members, the lower the litigation costs, and the more likely the NLRB is to rule favorably on the charge.[12] By affecting the probability that a charge will be successful, NLRB doctrine influences the filing behavior of unions as well as the compliance behavior of employers. But only those employer actions that unions or workers choose to challenge can be seen.

Individual workers can also challenge employers' actions, and their filings have accounted for a significant part of the growth of regulatory litigation under the NLRA in the late 1950s and throughout the 1970s (chapter 3). Workers' charges may be instigated by their unions, who wish to involve them in the union's cause, to show the employer that the union is being pressed by the rank and file (particularly during collective bargaining) or to put pressure on the employer while disavowing the union's responsibility for the charge.

The fact that tactical considerations, rather than substantive or

11. The practical difficulties of restoring the status quo ante are discussed in chap. 2.

12. Myron Roomkin, "A Quantitative Study of Unfair Labor Practice Cases," *Industrial and Labor Relations Review,* vol. 34 (January 1981), pp. 251–54, found that between 1952 and 1975, unions were more likely to file charges against employers at times when a majority of the NLRB was appointed by a Democratic president.

qualitative differences in underlying conduct, may determine whether an individual rather than a union challenges employers' conduct suggests that workers, like unions, may balance expected gains against expected costs to determine whether or not to file a charge. A worker's incentive, like the union's, varies directly with the impact of the employer's labor relations behavior on pay or working conditions and the likelihood of a favorable ruling by the NLRA and inversely with litigation costs. Some of the surge of charges by individual workers should be traceable to these factors. (The possibility that changes in legal doctrine under the NLRA may have contributed to the increase in individual charges is explored later.)

Clearly the employer's choice of behavior depends in part on whether a union or a worker chooses to file a charge, and the choice on each side is influenced by expectations of NLRB rulings and by each party's reaction to the difference between union and nonunion wages. For example, the direct effect of an increase in the wage differential is to increase the employer's incentive to adopt potentially illegal behavior. The larger the differential, however, the stronger the incentive is for the union or its members to challenge the employer's behavior. The union's probable counteraction makes potentially illegal behavior on the employer's part more risky and thus less likely to be adopted. The strategic interaction between the parties produces important indirect incentives.

Unions and workers may choose not to file a charge because they believe the employer's behavior, while of questionable legality, will not have an important impact on labor relations outcomes. The very fact that some technical violations of the act are not challenged by the supposed victims may be revealing information that some NLRB rules are not relevant to the larger purposes of the act. Or the victims may not feel it is worth incurring even small litigation costs if a successful ruling by the NLRB is unlikely.

Regulatory Incentives and Employer Compliance

Compliance can be increased by raising the expected cost of noncompliance, including both the likelihood of detection and the costs incurred if a violation is detected. Indeed, economic analyses of law enforcement stress the trade-off between the probability of detection and the magnitude of punishment in deterring violations of the law. Theoretically a given level of compliance can be attained even when the likelihood of detection is low if penalties can be set sufficiently high.[13]

Although employers' calculus includes this trade-off between detection and punishment under the NLRA, there are important institutional limits to regulatory influence on each variable. First, the likelihood of detection is the probability that a union or worker will file a charge. The NLRB has no direct role in the filing of a charge but through its doctrinal decisions has an indirect influence on whether the victim finds it worth incurring the litigation costs of filing a charge. Second, since corrective measures under the NLRA must be remedial rather than punitive, the theoretical possibility of offsetting low probabilities of detection with high penalties is not available.

These limitations produce a startling result. Although an employer's compliance behavior is influenced in principle by the likelihood that a charge will be filed, a formal analysis of the incentive structure reveals that where there were no punitive fines, where the likelihood that the NLRB would sustain a charge was less than one, and where litigation costs were low, there was no likelihood that a union or worker would rationally file a charge that would induce employer compliance (see the appendix).[14] Given the present remedial setup, one of the most remarkable facts about the NLRA may be that there is any employer compliance at all. It is apparently the realization that incentives are almost nonexistent that has made amending the NLRA to permit punitive damages a staple of regulatory reform proposals in recent decades.[15] By increasing the expected costs of borderline or clearly noncompliant behavior, a punitive fine should raise employer compliance directly for any given level of detection. And if the fine were collected by the union, it should raise the expected benefit from filing an unfair labor practice charge and hence the likelihood that a charge would be filed. The probability of detection would increase, and the higher likelihood that a charge would be filed would feed back into the employer's compliance decision,

13. Becker, "Crime and Punishment"; A. Mitchell Polinsky, *An Introduction to Law and Economics* (Little, Brown, 1983), chap. 10.

14. Robert J. Flanagan, "Compliance and Enforcement Decisions Under the National Labor Relations Act" (Stanford University, Graduate School of Business, October 1986).

15. The proposed Labor Reform Act of 1977 would have awarded double their lost pay (with no mitigation for interim earnings) to illegally discharged workers. *Labor Reform Act of 1977*, H. Rept. 95-637, 95 Cong. 1 sess. (GPO, 1977), p. 58.

working against noncompliance. The policy choice between punitive and fully compensatory remedies is discussed further in chapter 6.

Union Compliance Decisions

A parallel analysis can be applied to explain the pattern of charges against unions, which has the following empirical features. Only a small proportion of all unfair labor practice charges is filed against unions; individual workers are more likely than employers to file such charges, and charges by individuals against unions have grown much more rapidly since 1970 than charges by employers (see chapter 3). Under the NLRA compliance process, charges against unions will be low to the extent that unions' incentive to adopt behavior of borderline legality is low and employers' and workers' incentive to challenge union behavior is low.

A union following a strategy of balancing the benefits and costs of complying with the NLRA is likely to consider adopting labor relations behavior of uncertain legality if it promises better benefits for members than behavior that is clearly legal. The union's decision is tempered by the knowledge that if an employer (or worker) challenges the action, the union will incur litigation costs. And if the NLRB sustains a charge of unfair labor practice, the union will also incur the cost of the remedy.

Therefore, a union is more likely to adopt behavior that is clearly in compliance with the NLRA when violating the act would have little impact on the benefits received by its members, when the probability of an adverse Board ruling is high, and when the likelihood that an employer or worker will file a charge against the union is high. An employer will have little incentive to file a charge if an infraction has little or no impact on labor costs and profitability or if a favorable ruling on the charge is unlikely. (The employer's decision will, of course, feed back to influence the union's compliance decision.) The fact that employers file few charges may signal that union violations of the NLRA have a small impact on labor relations outcomes. And the knowledge that secondary boycotts and similar union activities can be immediately halted by injunction undoubtedly encourages compliance.[16] A low likelihood of success has both a direct impact on the union's compliance decision and an indirect impact through its effect in raising the likelihood that an employer will file a charge.

16. Taft-Hartley Act, sec. 10.1, 61 Stat. 149 (1947).

Why then, during a period when comparatively few charges are brought by employers, should individual workers increasingly file charges against unions? The answer must rest on the fact that different areas of the NLRA pertain to the interests of workers and of employers, so that each party has different incentives to file charges. Union violations of some practices may have little influence on the extent of unionization or collective bargaining power, factors of concern to employers. But union violations of practices such as the duty of fair representation may have a considerable impact on the benefits received by individual workers that gives them an incentive to file charges. In addition, the likelihood of favorable rulings by the NLRB on issues of interest to employers may differ from that on issues of interest to individual workers.

Compliance Incentives

The analysis of strategic behavior within the regulatory framework established under the NLRA highlights two general types of incentives that appear to influence compliance decisions under the NLRA. The first are those that are produced by the regulatory system itself. The NLRB and courts, through their specific rulings, create expectations about the likelihood that various labor relations activities constitute a violation of the act. But these rulings themselves appear to be subject to political influence, and there is evidence that presidential appointments and the political leanings of congressional committees responsible for appropriations and oversight of the NLRB affect the pro-labor or pro-business mix of Board decisions.[17] The Board's decisions, by influencing the legality of behavior and hence the likelihood that unfair labor practice charges will be sustained, feed back into the compliance and filing decisions of the parties.

The consequences of being found in violation of the NLRA also influence compliance behavior. Here, the most important feature of the act (as noted in chapter 2) is the remedial character of corrective measures. Rarely is the status quo in labor relations at the time of an infringement restored, which has prompted the periodic pressure for labor law reform.[18]

17. Terry M. Moe, "Control and Feedback in Economic Regulation: The Case of the NLRB," *American Political Science Review*, vol. 79 (December 1985), pp. 1094–1116.
18. Some remedies that have been applied by the Board and approved by the courts

The second type of incentive that has an influence on strategic behavior emanates from the general economic environment and results of collective bargaining. These are factors outside the Board's direct control. To the extent that the degree of compliance influences labor costs, changes in the relative cost of compliance may influence the volume of litigation.

Empirical Analysis of Compliance and Enforcement

The growth in unfair labor practice charges against employers (the vast majority of charges filed under the NLRA) can be examined by testing for the predicted relationships between the incentives determining compliance and enforcement and the number of unfair practice charges. Charges against employers can increase because a larger fraction of employers decides to behave strategically, a larger proportion chooses labor relations behavior of questionable legality, or the probability that a union challenges employer behavior increases. The empirical analysis focuses on the last two factors.

It is clear from the preceding analysis that a strategic employer's compliance choice depends in part on the union's enforcement choice and that both are influenced by the past record of NLRB decisions, which indicates the likelihood that a charge will be successful. Consideration of a specific example—the effect of the difference in employer labor costs (union benefits) associated with activities that may violate the act—may clarify the important interdependence. When the difference in benefits associated with possible noncompliance increases, unions and workers have a strong incentive to charge that an unfair labor practice has occurred, even when the odds of success with the NLRB are low. Even if employers did not alter their labor relations behavior, the number of charges would increase because unions and workers were more likely to challenge existing behavior.

But the increase in labor costs associated with compliance also has both direct and indirect effects on the employer's compliance choice. The direct effect is to increase an employer's incentive to choose risky behavior (in order to reduce expected labor costs) even when the odds that a charge will be filed are high. This raises the number of charges.

---

impart a penalty in the sense of raising an employer's costs—for example, requiring an employer to give back pay to a worker who was discharged because of union activity and replaced with another worker.

The indirect effect is to avoid risky behavior because the likelihood that a charge will be filed by a union or worker has risen. This reduces the number of charges. Absent exceptional circumstances, the forces raising regulatory litigation as a result of the pay difference associated with uncertain compliance outweigh the forces decreasing litigation. The behavior of the specific compliance incentives is discussed below.

LABOR COST DIFFERENTIAL. The difference in wage costs incurred (from the employer's perspective) or incomes received (from the union and worker's perspective) as a result of compliance or noncompliance with the NLRA affects both compliance and enforcement incentives. Yet remarkably little is known about the direct relation between noncompliance and labor costs. What is known is that, on average, unionized workers have a 10–20 percent wage advantage over nonunionized workers (after controlling for factors such as worker quality and endogeneity of union status), there is considerable variation across industries in this wage differential, and the differential grew during the 1970s.[19] Also, it has been shown that while union firms may be more productive, unions generally reduce profitability.[20] The compensation effects outweigh the productivity effects.

The wage differential represents an average across all union and nonunion workers and may not reflect the incremental cost (or income, from the union or worker perspective) associated with the establishment of a new collective bargaining relationship. If unions rationally organize first those industries in which their power is greatest, for example, the marginal return from their efforts will decline. Newly established unions may not be able to negotiate the average union wage premium.[21]

19. For extensive discussions, critiques, and analyses of over two hundred studies, see H. G. Lewis, *Unionism and Relative Wages in the United States: An Empirical Inquiry* (University of Chicago Press, 1963), and *Union Relative Wage Effects: A Survey* (University of Chicago Press, 1986). Between 1969 and 1982 the gross union-nonunion wage differential (unadjusted for differences between sectors in the quality of workers) in manufacturing widened by 13.5 percentage points; Robert J. Flanagan, "Wage Concessions and Long-Term Union Wage Flexibility," *Brookings Papers on Economic Activity, 1:1984*, p. 187. See also George E. Johnson, "Changes Over Time in the Union-Nonunion Wage Differential in the United States," in Jean-Jacques Rosa, ed., *The Economics of Trade Unions: New Directions* (Boston: Kluwer-Nijhoff, 1984), pp. 3–19; Daniel J. B. Mitchell, *Unions, Wages, and Inflation* (Brookings, 1980).

20. Richard B. Freeman and James L. Medoff, *What Do Unions Do?* (Basic Books, 1984), chaps. 11, 12; Kim B. Clark, "Unionization and Firm Performance: The Impact on Profits, Growth, and Productivity," *American Economic Review*, vol. 74 (December 1984), pp. 893–919.

21. Richard B. Freeman and Morris M. Kleiner, "Union Organizing Drive Outcomes

Moreover, the use of union-nonunion wage comparisons to approximate the costs of (or returns to) compliance with the NLRA assumes that the level and quality of union representation is influenced by the extent of compliance. But as the controversial research discussed in chapter 4 indicates, illegal behavior by employers during representation elections may have little impact on the outcome of elections. Finally, once a union has become the certified bargaining representative, the wage differential is unlikely to be an exact measure of the effect of violations of the NLRA—violation of the duty-to-bargain requirement, for example. The conceptually appropriate measure would be the difference in the union wage with and without a violation, but no such measure is available. The use of a general measure of union-nonunion compensation differentials is equivalent to assuming that the effect of such violations is to leave members of an established union no better off than nonunion workers.

Measures of the average union-nonunion wage differential are therefore unlikely to describe the exact size of the labor cost differential associated with noncompliance. It is plausible to assume, however, that variations in the costs to employers (or income of union members) are positively correlated with variations in the observed average difference between union and nonunion wages. This assumption is maintained in the empirical analysis of unfair labor practice charges. Figure 5-1 shows the behavior of the series.

SIZE OF UNIT. Data on the number of workers affected by each alleged unfair labor practice do not exist. Nevertheless, much of the regulation under the NLRA pertains to representation elections, so that the average number of workers participating in representation elections is a good approximation for unit size. The size of election units has been declining over time, implying a reduced incentive to violate the act. Less is known about trends in the size of established collective bargaining relationships, but mergers of bargaining units and increases in multiemployer bargaining indicate that bargaining unit size may have increased over time.

PROBABILITY OF SUCCESS. That compliance and filing behavior will be influenced by the expected probability that an action violates the NLRA is hardly controversial. Precisely for this reason, the expected probability of success is rarely observed directly. The fact that the parties adjust their behavior to their perception of the Board's stance on an issue

---

from NLRB Elections During a Period of Economic Concessions," in Barbara D. Dennis, ed., *Proceedings of the Thirty-Ninth Annual Meeting of the Industrial Relations Research Association* (Madison, Wisc.: IRRA, forthcoming.).

Figure 5-1. Logarithmic Relation of Union to Nonunion Wage Rates, 1948–80

Log of union relative wage index

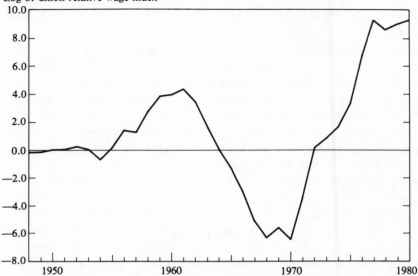

Source: George E. Johnson, "Changes Over Time in the Union-Nonunion Wage Differential in the United States," in Jean-Jacques Rosa, ed., *The Economics of Trade Unions: New Directions* (Boston: Kluwer-Nijhoff, 1984), pp. 3–19. Base year 1964 = 0.0.

means that many actual and potential disputes never receive Board action. Based on a reading of Board doctrine, some contemplated actions may never be taken, actions that are taken may not be challenged by the filing of unfair labor practice charges, and charges that are filed may be settled rather than adjudicated (when both parties share a common view about the general relationship between the facts of a dispute and the legal doctrines and decision standards of the NLRB and the reviewing courts). Only disputes in which the relationship of the facts to current NLRB doctrine is less clear to each party will cases be pressed to Board adjudication. Over a large number of adjudicated cases, however, about half of the rulings should be favorable to each side.[22] However, this observed win rate will differ from the theoretical probability of success confronting the parties when they make their compliance and enforcement decisions to the extent that the mix of cases reaching adjudication is altered by these decisions.

The main deviation from the observed 50 percent win rate should be

22. Priest and Klein, "Selection of Disputes for Litigation"; Moe, "Control and Feedback."

in periods in which the prevailing legal doctrine and decisional standards are changing. And these are most likely to be when the political party in power has changed and the new president is making appointments to the Board. For a short time the proportion of rulings favoring labor should shift (the direction depending on whether a pro-labor or pro-management shift in the Board has occurred), and the observed win rate should be closest to the theoretical probability of success. Once compliance, filing, and settlement behavior has adjusted to the new doctrinal position of the Board, the win rate should revert to about 50 percent, even though the theoretical probability of success is unchanged.[23]

The fact that the theoretical probability of success with the NLRB is rarely observable raises challenging problems of measurement. The empirical analysis exploits the fact that shifts in legal doctrine are most likely when the political party in power has changed. The probability of success is assumed to shift with the political affiliation of a majority of the Board members. (Technically, the proxy is a dummy variable taking the value one in years that Democrats constitute a majority of the NLRB and zero otherwise.) This measure is not subject to the problems that adaptive behavior may raise for observed win rates, although it imposes the assumption that the probability of success remains unchanged during periods in which either party has a majority. The role of this variable is compared to that of a measure of the win rate—the proportion of pro-labor decisions handed down by the NLRB.

REMEDIES. The remedial authority of the NLRB, as noted in chapter 2, is limited to rectifying the harm done to individual workers as a result of unfair labor practices and to restoring the status quo in labor relations at the time that a violation occurred. The two concepts are not the same, for actions against individual workers often affect the desire to unionize among a larger group of workers. Nevertheless, there is a question of whether the growth of regulatory litigation under the NLRA is related to remedial awards by the NLRB.

This question can be addressed by examining remedial actions for one of the harshest unfair labor practices—discharge of a worker because of union activities. The standard remedy for a proven violation is reinstatement of the discharged worker with back pay. Trends in nominal back pay awarded to illegally discharged employees are reported in figure 5-2. The average award to each worker increased substantially

---

23. Moe, "Control and Feedback," pp. 1106–07.

Figure 5-2. Back Pay Awarded to Illegally Discharged Employees, 1948–80

Dollars per employee

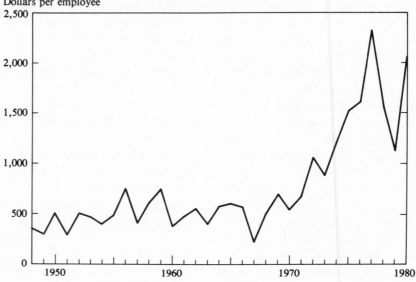

Source: National Labor Relations Board, Office of Statistical Services.

during the 1970s at the same time that violations (measured by the number of workers receiving awards) were increasing. Superficially, it appears that noncompliance increased as violations became more expensive.

Nominal awards for back pay are based on lost earnings (with interest) for the period following the illegal discharge, mitigated by earnings received from any intervening jobs. Earnings and interest rates respond in part to inflation, so that increases in this determinant of back pay are unlikely to increase the remedial burden on an employer so long as the employer's product prices are closely correlated with a general index of prices. The actual burden could change, however, with variations in the degree of mitigation. Mitigation is determined by the availability of alternative jobs and workers' willingness to accept them. Job availability should vary inversely with the unemployment rate.

In order to explore the paradox noted above, the average nominal back pay awarded per discharged worker, *BACKPAY*, was related to average hourly earnings, *WAGE;* average earnings interacted with the unemployment rate, *WAGE*UR*, in order to test for mitigation; the interest rate on three-month Treasury bills, *TBILL3;* and a time trend, *TIME*, in a multiple regression analysis. A regression on annual data for

1948–80 finds that remedial awards are strongly influenced by the growth of nominal wages and, consistent with the cyclical variation in opportunities for mitigation, the wage element of back pay awards is larger when unemployment is high.[24] There is also a puzzling negative relation to the three-month Treasury bill rate that may reflect the NLRB's very slow adjustment to rising interest rates, particularly during the 1970s. Once this factor is controlled for, there is no significant time trend in back pay awards by the Board. It appears that there has been no change in the Board's remedial policy over the period. For the most part the growth in nominal penalties reflects the rapid growth of wages during the 1970s, which largely reflects the inflation of the period. The real values of back pay awards tend to track real wages, and there is no indication of an increasing burden on employers generally. However, those employers whose product prices do not keep up with prices generally may see an increased burden in the growth of back pay awards.

DELAYS IN ADJUDICATION. Unfair labor practices often have direct private effects on individual parties (those discharged for union activities) and external effects on the larger venture (the union representation campaign or collective bargaining negotiations) of which the individual action is a part. Delays in adjudication increase the effect on collective processes (see chapter 4), which gives employers an incentive to reduce compliance when delays are long. Aside from its direct effects, additional litigation challenging an employer's behavior adds to the congestion and delays. The average number of days to a Board hearing has varied dramatically over the postwar period, but has increased substantially since the mid-1970s (figure 5-3).

Unions' Charges against Employers

In order to explore how the growth of regulatory litigation varies with the incentives to comply with and enforce the NLRA, several regressions

---

24. The regression estimate is

$$BACKPAY = -40.39 + 16.99 \ WAGE + 1.29 \ WAGE*UR - 70.58 \ TBILL3 - 7.60 \ TIME.$$
$$\quad\quad\quad (0.39) \quad (2.13) \quad\quad\quad (1.70) \quad\quad\quad\quad (1.71) \quad\quad\quad (0.63)$$

$$\bar{R}^2 = 0.83; \ \text{Durbin-Watson statistic} = 2.20$$

The numbers in parentheses are t-statistics and $\bar{R}^2$ is the coefficient of determination adjusted for degrees of freedom. Data for the wage variable (the adjusted hourly earnings index for private nonagricultural workers, where 1977 = 100) and the interest rate on three-month Treasury bills are from *Economic Report of the President, February 1985*, pp. 276, 310. The unemployment rate series was provided by George L. Perry.

**Figure 5-3. Average Number of Days between Filing of Unfair Labor Practice
Charge and NLRB Adjudication, 1950–80**

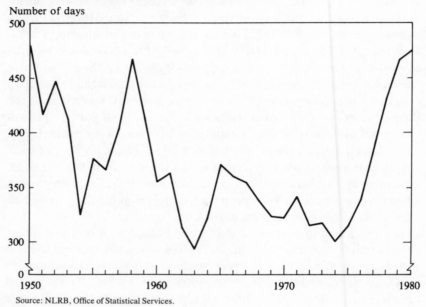

Source: NLRB, Office of Statistical Services.

were estimated on annual data for 1950–80. The variables tested and the
results of regression analyses of unfair labor practice charges filed by
unions against employers are reported in table 5-2. In regression 1, the
signs on the variables are as predicted, but there is a decidedly mixed
pattern of statistical significance. Increases in the union relative wage
and growth in the size of bargaining units produce a significant increase
in charges filed by unions against employers. As expected, the remedial
philosophy behind the NLRB's back pay awards does not have a reliable
deterrent effect. Even the measure of delays in reaching NLRB decisions
falls short of conventional standards of significance. But charges by
unions against employers are significantly higher in years when a majority
of the Board members are Democrats. The NLRB obviously influences
the volume of litigation through its doctrinal standards. Despite the
significant time trend, the low Durbin-Watson statistic suggests that
something is missing from an analysis based solely on compliance
incentives.

   An obvious candidate is a measure of labor relations activity. With
the addition of the number of union representation elections, in regres-

Table 5-2. Regressions of Unfair Labor Practice Charges by Unions against Employers, 1950–80

Variable	Regression number[a]					
	1	*2*	*3*	*4*	*5*	*6*[b]
Constant term	−7,883	−11,443	−11,398	−10,311	−10,698	−13,958
	(5.12)	(6.37)	(6.42)	(4.69)	(4.88)	(5.61)
Union-nonunion wage differential, *RELWAGE*	204.56	221.69	210.90	177.60	208.52	154.74
	(4.20)	(5.19)	(5.40)	(4.90)	(4.39)	(2.83)
Number of workers in election unit, *SIZE*	52.07	53.94	52.42	54.98	50.70	40.75
	(4.16)	(4.95)	(4.97)	(5.21)	(4.63)	(2.99)
Real back pay awarded per discharged worker, *BPAY*	0.15	−0.76	. . .	. . .	. . .	. . .
	(0.12)	(0.67)				
Days between filing and decision, *DELAY*	0.86	4.27	4.14	6.75	3.15	12.64
	(0.23)	(1.23)	(1.21)	(2.13)	(0.85)	(2.01)
Democratic majority on NLRB, *DEM*	1,237	758.34	855.51	. . .	859.66	515.72
	(3.66)	(2.26)	(2.87)		(2.69)	(1.33)
Proportion of pro-labor rulings by NLRB, *NLRB*	. . .	. . .	. . .	68.01	. . .	. . .
				(1.58)		
Time trend, *TIME*	550.37	488.40	486.61	457.41	467.80	463.55
	(18.65)	(14.77)	(14.94)	(13.73)	(11.67)	(11.92)
Number of representation elections, *ELEC*	. . .	0.54	0.51	0.80	0.49	0.65
		(2.97)	(2.93)	(5.09)	(2.67)	(3.07)
Rate of unemployment adjusted for demographic changes in labor force, *UR*	. . .	. . .	. . .	. . .	7.14	. . .
					(0.04)	
Rate of change of consumer price index, *CPI*	. . .	. . .	. . .	. . .	56.61	. . .
					(0.98)	
Summary statistic						
$\bar{R}^{2}$ [c]	0.97	0.98	0.98	0.98	0.98	0.97
Durbin-Watson	1.39	1.71	1.71	1.42	1.54	1.57
Standard error of estimate	768	667	660	647	674	739

Sources: NLRB, Office of Statistical Services; George E. Johnson, "Changes Over Time in the Union-Nonunion Wage Differential in the United States," in Jean-Jacques Rosa, ed., *The Economics of Trade Unions: New Directions* (Boston: Kluwer-Nijhoff, 1984), pp. 3–19; Terry M. Moe, "Control and Feedback in Economic Regulation: The Case of the NLRB," *American Political Science Review*, vol. 79 (December 1985), pp. 1094–1116; *Annual Report of the NLRB*, various years.

a. Regression coefficients and related test statistics are from variants on the regression model estimated on annual data for 1950–80:

$$UE_t = a_0 + a_1\,RELWAGE_t + a_2\,SIZE_t + a_3\,BPAY_t + a_4\,DELAY_t + a_5\,DEM_t + a_6\,TIME_t + e,$$

where UE_t is the number of unfair labor practice charges filed by unions against employers in year t, e is the error, and the other variables are as defined in the table. Numbers in parentheses are t-statistics.

b. Results of two-stage least-squares regression.

c. Coefficient of determination adjusted for degrees of freedom.

sion 2, the substantive and statistical results of the regression improve markedly. While representation elections have a significant effect on charges filed, there is a substantial additional influence from the variables representing compliance and enforcement incentives. The coefficients in regression 2 indicate that on average a 1 percent increase in the union-nonunion wage differential is associated with an increase of about 220 unfair practice charges by unions against employers each year. The earlier theoretical analysis indicates that the increase reflects the direct effect of the increased wage differential on employer behavior; the effect on the union's decision to file more charges is canceled by the feedback into the employer's decisions. Similarly, a 10-person increase in the average election (bargaining) unit size induces changes in employer behavior that result in about 540 additional unfair practice charges per year by unions.

Real back pay per discharged employee and adjudication time still fall short of conventional standards of statistical significance. The back pay variable is so unpromising that it is omitted from the remaining regressions in table 5-2. This deletion produces negligible change in the role of the compliance and labor relations variables (regression 3). A variable for the proportion of pro-labor rulings in cases reaching the NLRB for adjudication is not statistically significant when it is substituted for the variable indicating the political composition of the Board as a proxy for the probability that charges filed against employers will be successful (regression 4). As a measure of the win rate, this variable is polluted by the effects of adaptive behavior by unions and employers.

The ordinary least-squares regressions do not correct for possible simultaneous relationships between unfair labor practice charges and some of the explanatory variables in the analysis. In particular, while delays in adjudication may influence regulatory litigation, the volume of litigation may also produce congestion that contributes to the delays. In order to correct for possible simultaneous-equations bias, regression 3 was reestimated by two-stage least squares. The results are reported as regression 6.[25] The results parallel the estimates by ordinary least squares with two exceptions: increases in the period of adjudication now raise charges by unions against employers, but the presence of a Democratic majority on the Board is no longer a significant influence on charges.

25. Delays in adjudication are a function of the volume of regulatory litigation and the level of resources available to process it. Therefore, variables representing appropriations for several NLRB functions were used as instrumental variables along with the exogenous variables in the regression explaining unfair labor practice charges.

Workers' Charges against Employers

For purely tactical reasons, charges may be filed against an employer by individual workers rather than by a union. In instances where workers file charges as surrogates for unions, the same set of incentives should influence the behavior of each party. The regressions reported in table 5-3 thus apply the same compliance incentives to charges filed by workers against employers that table 5-2 applies to charges filed by unions. The results indicate that some charges by workers are sensitive to compliance incentives, which is consistent with the idea that tactical considerations are an important determinant of the choice of filing party. The effects of wage differences, delays in adjudication of NLRB decisions, and size of the election unit are all significant. (The somewhat larger quantitative effect of the size of the unit on charges filed by unions may reflect their greater interest in organizationwide issues.) As in table 5-2, real back pay awards are an insignificant remedy in the regressions in table 5-3.

In three respects, however, the results in table 5-3 differ from the results in table 5-2. First, charges filed by individual workers are not significantly related to the number of representation elections. For a given set of incentives, an employer's failure to comply during representation elections is more likely to be challenged by unions than by individual workers. Second, the time trend is smaller for charges filed by workers than for charges filed by unions, suggesting that the extension of rights to individual workers under the NLRA (discussed in chapter 2) has not been an unusually large independent source of the unexplained growth of the charges against employers. Finally, charges filed by workers appear to be unaffected by either measure of the probability of success with the NLRB. This may be because individual workers are less likely to be informed of changes in NLRB doctrine than union organizations. The idea is more persuasive, however, for filings in which workers are not merely acting as substitutes for their unions. The two-stage estimate produces little change in the results for charges filed by workers (regression 6).

Competing Explanations of Regulatory Litigation

The regulatory puzzle developed in chapter 3 was the fact that unfair labor practice charges have increased relative to the number of representation elections and to other regulated activity. The empirical results reported above show that much, although not all, of the puzzle can be

Table 5-3. Regressions of Unfair Labor Practice Charges by Workers against Employers, 1950–80

Variable	Regression number[a]					
	1	*2*	*3*	*4*	*5*	*6*[b]
Constant term	−6,692	−6,988	−7,034	−5,596	−7,503	−7,687
	(6.42)	(4.90)	(4.96)	(3.11)	(4.35)	(4.28)
Union-nonunion wage differential, *RELWAGE*	225.80	227.23	238.21	248.41	215.29	223.89
	(6.85)	(6.70)	(7.63)	(8.37)	(5.76)	(5.67)
Number of workers in election unit, *SIZE*	18.09	18.25	19.80	21.46	18.01	16.83
	(2.14)	(2.11)	(2.35)	(2.48)	(2.09)	(1.71)
Average back pay awarded per discharged worker, *BPAY*	0.85	0.78	. . .	. . .	. . .	. . .
	(1.00)	(0.86)				
Days between filing and decision, *DELAY*	7.48	7.76	7.89	7.76	7.90	10.06
	(2.92)	(2.81)	(2.88)	(3.00)	(2.70)	(2.22)
Democratic majority on NLRB, *DEM*	43.25	3.45	−95.45	. . .	−13.03	−182.07
	(0.19)	(0.01)	(0.40)		(0.05)	(0.65)
Proportion of pro-labor rulings by NLRB, *NLRB*	. . .	. . .	. . .	−33.29	. . .	. . .
				(0.95)		
Time trend, *TIME*	372.19	367.03	368.86	376.56	349.12	362.98
	(18.65)	(13.99)	(14.18)	(13.80)	(11.07)	(12.93)
Number of representation elections, *ELEC*	. . .	0.04	0.08	0.07	0.11	0.11
		(0.31)	(0.57)	(0.57)	(0.76)	(0.75)
Rate of unemployment adjusted for demographic changes in labor force, *UR*	. . .	. . .	. . .	. . .	146.02	. . .
					(1.11)	
Rate of change of consumer price index, *CPI*	. . .	. . .	. . .	. . .	33.25	. . .
					(0.73)	
Summary statistic						
$\bar{R}^2$ [c]	0.98	0.98	0.98	0.98	0.98	0.98
Durbin-Watson	1.61	1.67	1.71	1.67	1.67	1.74
Standard error of estimate	520	530	527	530	531	533

Sources: Same as table 5-2.

a. Regression coefficients and related test statistics are from variants on the regression model estimated on annual data for 1950–80:

$$IE_t = b_0 + b_1\,RELWAGE_t + b_2\,SIZE_t + b_3\,BPAY_t + b_4\,DELAY_t + b_5\,DEM_t + b_6\,TIME_t + e_t\,,$$

where IE_t is the number of unfair labor practice charges filed by individual workers against employers in year t, e is the error, and the other variables are as defined in the table. Numbers in parentheses are t-statistics.

b. Results of two-stage least-squares regression.

c. Coefficient of determination adjusted for degrees of freedom.

explained by the effects of changing compliance and enforcement incentives on strategic behavior. Do these incentives play a stronger role in explaining the puzzle than changes in the volume of economic activity?

Regression 5 in tables 5-2 and 5-3 explores this question. It expands the explanatory variables in regression 3 to include the aggregate unemployment and inflation rates. Clearly, the models based on compliance incentives fit better than the expanded versions in terms of the usual statistical criteria. In each table the influence of the macroeconomic variables is decisively rejected. Neither the unemployment rate nor the inflation rate attains conventional standards of statistical significance in either of the regressions. The economywide influences on regulatory litigation that some of the analyses discussed in chapter 3 point to appear to be an artifact of underlying changes in compliance incentives.

Why Do U.S. Employers Resist Unions?

The United States is not the only country in which union wages increased substantially during the 1970s. In most European countries, for example, the growth of union wages following the oil price shocks is one of the main reasons advanced for the growth of unemployment since the mid-1970s.[26] Yet the opposition of employers to unions appears to be much greater in the United States than in Europe.

The differences in resistance to unions should reflect differences in the expected effect of a union on an employer's competitive position. For a number of reasons, including some that are related to the design and implementation of labor policy, union actions appear to pose more of a threat to the competitive position of employers in the United States than in Europe. The effects of unions on wages appear to present a greater competitive threat to American employers largely because of international differences in bargaining structure.[27] Bargaining in the United States is more likely to be established at the plant or company

26. Michael Bruno and Jeffrey D. Sachs, *Economics of Worldwide Stagflation* (Harvard University Press, 1985), chap. 9; Robert J. Flanagan, David W. Soskice, and Lloyd Ulman, *Unionism, Economic Stabilization, and Incomes Policies: European Experience* (Brookings, 1983).

27. Lewis, *Union Relative Wage Effects.*

level than at the regional, industry, or even nationwide level.[28] With decentralized collective bargaining, employers cannot be assured that the costs they incur under union contracts will be matched by their competitors, either union or nonunion. Thus, the incentive to violate the NLRA as a method of resisting a threat to their competitive position may be strong.

This source of resistance to unions and of regulatory litigation is itself traceable in part to the policies developed under the NLRA—in particular to election procedures that sometimes result in votes for union representation by work groups that would not have the power to organize by other means. The influence of the NLRB's unit determination policies (see chapter 2) is less certain. In its effort to define communities of interest that are appropriate for collective bargaining, the Board has identified increasingly smaller units. While the smaller average unit size may arguably increase the threat of competition and contribute to employer resistance, the regression results reported in tables 5-2 and 5-3 indicate that smaller unit size is associated with fewer charges of employer unfair labor practices.

Relatively centralized bargaining structures are only one of the institutional arrangements that insulate European employers from fear of union wage increases. Unionized competitors tend to face the same wage rates, and laws requiring an extension of negotiated wages to the unorganized sector in some countries require the nonunion sector to adopt the negotiated wage level. Labor policies therefore tend to reduce the competitive threat presented by union wage increases.[29]

Unions in the United States also secure relatively high fringe benefits for their members, which increases the competitive threat from the nonunion sector.[30] In addition, decentralized bargaining may result in

28. In the United States there are over 150,000 labor agreements. More than half of the agreements in manufacturing covering at least 1,000 workers are negotiated at the plant level, with close to 90 percent being between a union and a single employer. Outside of manufacturing, multiemployer agreements are more common but usually are limited to local product markets. Bureau of Labor Statistics, *Characteristics of Major Collective Bargaining Agreements, January 1, 1980,* bulletin 2095 (GPO, 1981), p. 19.

29. European employers (and their workers) remain exposed to foreign competitive pressures. But because institutional arrangements tend to spread union wage effects throughout the economy, the response is likely to be pressure by both labor and management on government to accommodate cost increases via fiscal policy or devaluation. See Lars Calmfors and Henrik Horn, "Classical Unemployment, Accommodation Policies and the Adjustment of Real Wages," *Scandinavian Journal of Economics,* vol. 87, no. 2 (1985), pp. 234–61.

30. Richard B. Freeman, "The Effect of Unionism on Fringe Benefits," *Industrial and Labor Relations Review,* vol. 34 (July 1981), pp. 489–509.

differences in fringe benefit costs within the unionized sector. In Europe most fringe benefits are established by law and hence apply with relatively equal force to most employers. International differences in the division of responsibilities between legislation and collective bargaining therefore influence the competitive threat associated with unions.

During the 1970s, American management resistance to unionization was reinforced by a confluence of events that resulted in substantial increases in the competitive pressures in several traditionally unionized industries. In the airline and trucking industries, deregulation removed barriers to entry into industries with a basically competitive market structure, and competition from new, often nonunion, firms increased. In the highly unionized smokestack industries, foreign producers took an increasing share of American markets, by 1980 accounting for 22 percent of the U.S. automobile market, an increase of 83 percent over the import share in 1970. During the 1970s, import shares more than doubled in the apparel, nonferrous metal, textile, footwear, and metal machinery industries.[31] Empirically, pressure on profits is associated with more unfair labor practice charges against employers.[32]

Resistance to unions is only one strategy that employers may adopt if they wish to remain nonunion. And it may not be the most productive strategy, since most workers appear to base their unionization choice on factors related to job satisfaction that are determined long before their ballot is cast. Some students of industrial relations believe that much of the growth of the nonunion sector reflects efforts by increasing numbers of employers to adopt human resource management methods that are designed to raise job satisfaction and to motivate and reward workers individually.[33] This is yet another reason why trends in aggregate membership tend to have no connection with developments in the regulatory system.

Strategic Behavior and the Volume of Litigation

The analysis of strategic interactions between the parties to labor relations and the NLRB provides several insights into the litigation

31. Flanagan, "Wage Concessions," p. 184.
32. Robert J. Flanagan, "Remedial Policy and Compliance with the NLRA," in Dennis, ed., *Proceedings of the Thirty-Ninth Annual Meeting.*
33. Thomas A. Kochan, Robert B. McKersie, and Harry C. Katz, "U.S. Industrial Relations in Transition: A Summary Report," in Barbara D. Dennis, ed., *Proceedings of the Thirty-Seventh Annual Meeting of the Industrial Relations Research Association* (Madison, Wisc.: IRRA, 1985), pp. 261–76.

explosion described in chapter 3. First, although the volume of regulated labor relations activity in the United States has some influence on the volume of regulatory litigation (in the case of representation elections, only on charges filed by unions), much of the growth in unfair labor practice charges depends on compliance and enforcement incentives.

Second, the analysis confirms the meager incentives for employer compliance under the present remedial policies of the NLRB. Thus, the Board would have further influence if it were able to fashion fully compensatory or punitive damages. This issue is discussed further in chapter 6. Third, the Board's rulings have less influence on unfair labor practice charges than is commonly supposed.

The volume of regulatory litigation is sensitive also to administrative actions of the NLRB and to budgeting decisions of Congress that influence the speed with which charges are adjudicated. The empirical analysis in this chapter confirms those studies that suggest that delays in adjudication influence the outcome of representation elections and other protected activity, and the making of compliance and enforcement decisions.

Some of the outcomes of the regulatory approach to public policy on labor relations are more or less independent of the actions taken by the regulatory agency. This is because the compliance and enforcement choices that determine the volume of unfair labor practice charges are influenced in part by incentives that are determined in the market and through collective bargaining. Indeed, the larger lesson of the analysis of compliance decisions and the links between union representation and unfair labor practices is that the effect of NLRB policy on labor relations outcomes is often swamped by factors that are beyond its sphere of influence. In particular, the sustained growth of the unions' wage advantage during the 1970s, by reducing the incentives of employers to comply with the NLRA and increasing the incentives of unions to challenge potentially illegal behavior, appears to have had a profound influence on the growth of unfair labor practice charges. It is easy to see how damage awards aimed at increasing compliance and reducing regulatory litigation at the margin could be similarly overwhelmed in the aggregate by other economic incentives.

While the explanations developed in this chapter are more enlightening than analyses that simply relate unfair labor practice charges to measures of labor relations activity, they leave an unexplained gap between regulatory litigation and labor relations activity in the 1970s. The regression analysis does not capture possible extensions in the rights protected under the NLRA (chapter 2) that could produce more charges from a given volume of activity. Moreover, the proportion of employers that behave strategically toward the act may have shifted.

In addition, shifts in tastes could produce changes in the volume of regulatory litigation. They could include purely ideological shifts in attitudes toward unions that influence employer compliance with the NLRA (again outside the economic calculus of compliance discussed in this chapter). They could also include shifts in attitudes regarding the extent to which the legal system ought to protect certain rights that influence the proclivity to file charges. The general explosion in litigation may reflect social attitudes that have something to do with the increase in charges of unfair practice relative to regulated labor relations activity. Nevertheless, the research reported in this chapter strongly cautions against accepting such an idea without first analyzing the underlying choices that produce litigation. How to test the unexplored possibilities for their potential influence remains to be discovered.

CHAPTER 6

Alternative Policies toward Labor Relations

THE EXPLOSION of litigation under the National Labor Relations Act has imposed significant resource costs on both private parties and the public treasury. The act is believed to influence certain statutory rights accorded labor and management—such as the right to concerted action by employees—and broad social trends—such as the extent of union representation among workers in private nonagricultural jobs. It is also widely believed that the central factor in these developments is the actions of the regulatory agency that administers the statute, the National Labor Relations Board. Analysis of the nature and consequences of NLRA litigation, however, suggests that the common wisdom must be qualified.

One of the most striking features of the growth of regulatory litigation under the NLRA is its breadth. With unfair labor practice charges rising in every category of the law and among all parties to labor relations, the growth of litigation cannot be traced to a few key changes in legal doctrine under the act. Nor can much of the growth of charges be explained either by changes in the volume of labor relations activity (including changes resulting from the expansion of the NLRB's jurisdiction over time) or by changes in the regional and industrial distribution of labor relations activities, unemployment, and inflation. Instead, strategic interactions between the parties subject to regulation prove to be an important element in the broad-based growth of litigation. The NLRB is not a neutral force in this process, for its decisions influence the expectations of the parties to labor relations about the likely outcome of unfair practice charges. The Board's decisions thus feed back into the compliance and enforcement decisions of the parties that culminate in unfair practice charges. And yet the Board's influence can be dwarfed by incentives that are beyond its control—for example, by the kind of economic developments that account for much of the surge of regulatory litigation since the late 1950s.

Some violations of the NLRA may alter labor relations outcomes, but it is delays in adjudication—often caused by the congestion of regulatory litigation—that more consistently interfere with attainment of the objectives of the act. Moreover, unfair labor practices do not have a significant influence on aggregate union membership trends when compared with market adjustments to the rise in union wages relative to nonunion wages. In sum, labor policy, as administered through the NLRA, appears to have a decidedly secondary influence on both the growth of regulatory litigation and the consequences of that growth. Thus the possibilities for bringing about broad improvements in labor relations through changes in labor policy are rather circumscribed. But the fact that determinations under the NLRA may have little influence on unionization does not mean that the shape of public policy toward labor relations is irrelevant. A society may be concerned about guaranteeing certain rights as a part of the employment relationship quite apart from the effect of those rights on labor relations outcomes.

The distinction between rights and outcomes is of particular importance to the discussion of labor relations policy. Most assessments of economic regulation use the structure and behavior of competitive markets as a touchstone for policy action. By this criterion, public policies that may reduce competition in labor markets—and the NLRA is one such policy—are automatically suspect. The limits of policy discussion are relatively narrow, and deregulation is the favored policy choice.

An alternative frame of reference, and the one adopted in this study, holds that Congress, in passing the NLRA in 1935 with full knowledge of a long-standing antitrust policy, made a deliberate choice to accord workers certain rights, despite the fact that the exercise of those rights could result in anticompetitive outcomes. From this perspective, the question becomes how close existing policies and alternatives to those policies come to providing the rights guaranteed by the NLRA. This chapter discusses suggestions for revision of national labor policy, focusing first on changes in the existing regulatory framework and then on complete deregulation of labor relations.

Policy Alternatives under the Present Framework

Until recently, most proposals for reform were directed at increasing the effectiveness of the unfair labor practice provisions of the NLRA. Most of the proposals would either alter the remedial policies under the act, introduce procedural changes to reduce the opportunities for committing unfair labor practices, or make changes in the substantive doctrines of the NLRB.

Penalties

Expanding the NLRB's remedial authority to permit punitive actions has been a staple of regulatory reform proposals in recent decades. The proposed Labor Reform Act of 1977 would have doubled the lost pay (with no mitigation for interim earnings) awarded to workers who had been discharged illegally.[1] Other proposals for reform would have awarded treble damages (as in antitrust actions) or denied government contracts to firms guilty of egregious violations of the NLRA.

PUNITIVE FINES. A basic economic principle of legal remedies is that the optimal fine should be set equal to the costs the violation imposes on victims adjusted upward for the probability that violators will avoid detection and conviction.[2] Remedies based on this long-recognized principle encourage compliance whenever the private gains from violating the NLRA are less than the losses by all workers affected by the violation. Only when the private gains to the violator exceed the external costs of the activity are violations of labor relations law likely to occur. The size of the punitive element of any fine optimally varies with the likelihood of detection. Economic analysis therefore stresses that there are two elements to the design of remedial policy—damages to victims and the probability of detection—and that the second provides the rationale for punitive damages.

The objective of the NLRA is to encourage—not to require—the establishment of collective bargaining relationships. Illegal actions alter the expected gain from the legislation by changing the probability of

1. *Labor Reform Act of 1977*, H. Rept. 95-637, 95 Cong. 1 sess. (Government Printing Office, 1977), p. 58.
2. Gary S. Becker, "Crime and Punishment: An Economic Approach," *Journal of Political Economy*, vol. 76 (March–April 1968), pp. 169–217.

establishing a union or a collective bargaining contract. Therefore, the optimal fine would equal the change in the expected gain from unionization as a result of the violation. A remedy that effectively restores the status quo is perfectly consistent with this principle, for such a remedy would return the probabilities of unionization or of establishing a collective bargaining contract to where they were at the time of the violation. Thus, the difficulty with the current remedial approach under the NLRA is less with the concept—restoration of the status quo in labor relations at the time a violation occurred—than with its implementation.

Corrective actions that seek to rectify the harm suffered by individual workers ignore the external effects of violations on the general effort to pursue concerted activity. For example, restoration of employment (with back pay) to an illegally discharged worker is unlikely to address the effect that his discharge had on the general inclination to organize a union, particularly if the remedy occurs long after the discharge and the worker refuses reinstatement (as typically happens). Failure to incorporate external effects in the compensatory remedial approach of the NLRA means that enforcement, which must be initiated by the victims, will be too low. This point apparently motivates some proposals for punitive damages under the NLRA, although it is in fact an argument for fully compensatory remedies.

Obviously it is difficult to design a remedy for such offenses. The remedy would vary with the extent to which a violation interfered with workers' rights under the NLRA. But, as noted in chapter 4, this itself is a matter of controversy. The actual impact of violations of the act apparently ranges from zero to potentially serious interference. Setting a penalty equal to the external effects of a violation would in many instances require determining the substantive gains that workers would receive from collective bargaining. Unions have proposed such an approach to remedy employer violations of the duty to bargain. The Supreme Court has rejected such a remedy, however, on the grounds that to compel agreement over an issue would violate the basic premise of the act that the government should not be involved in determining the substantive outcome of collective bargaining.[3] The Board has therefore concluded that it does not have the authority to impose remedies that require an employer to reimburse employees for contract benefits that might have been obtained but for the refusal-to-bargain violation.[4]

3. *H.K. Porter Co.* v. *NLRB*, 397 U.S. 99 (1970).
4. *Ex-Cell-O Corp.*, 185 N.L.R.B. 107 (1970).

The traditional case for punitive damages rests on the difficulty of detecting and prosecuting a violation. The likelihood that unfair labor practices will be detected is high, since the behavior of all parties is easily observable. Given the low litigation costs faced by plaintiffs, unfair labor practice charges should be filed against violations causing compensable damage. When charges are promptly adjudicated, the standard case for punitive damages is therefore difficult to establish for violations of the NLRA except in two situations. One is when lengthy periods of adjudication erode the ability to compensate fully for damages, so that the likelihood that a charge is filed declines, even when a violation produces damage. The other is when remedies that do not compensate for the external cost of a violation reduce the incentive to file a charge.

Despite easy observability, many violations of the act go unchallenged. Either many violations of NLRA rules are so inconsequential to the outcome of labor relations that they are not even challenged by the victims, or violations that have consequences are so poorly remedied under the NLRA that it is not worth incurring even the low costs of filing an unfair labor practice charge. If the former is the dominant reason, the availability of punitive damages payable to victims is likely to produce overenforcement of the law; charges are likely to be brought for activities that do no damage. If the latter is the dominant reason, there will be underenforcement of the law. Research on why so many violations are not challenged is badly needed.

Remedies are only one element of the package of incentives influencing compliance and litigation choices under the NLRA (see chapter 5). The effects of remedial policies and other incentives controlled by the NLRB may be swamped by the effects of changes in the labor cost differential associated with unionism and other factors that are beyond the Board's span of influence. Although a change in remedial policy might alter compliance choices, it could not guarantee a major change in the general level of compliance or of regulatory litigation.

DENIAL OF GOVERNMENT CONTRACTS. The proposed Labor Reform Act of 1977 contained a provision that would have prevented flagrant labor law violators from holding government contracts for at least three years.[5] This proposal is similar in spirit to the use of government contract privileges as leverage to seek compliance with affirmative action goals, pay and price standards, and other government policies. The basic flaw

5. *Labor Reform Act of 1977*, H. Rept. 95-637, p. 58.

in this type of policy is its failure to take account of how the interaction between government and the contractor sector affects the noncontractor sector.

The proportionate change in compliance with the NLRA attributable to the prospect of denial of contracting rights consists of (1) the proportionate change in compliance that would have occurred in the absence of a debarment remedy (that is, as a result of nonpolicy influences), plus (2) the proportion of firms that are subject to the remedy because of their status as government contractors, multiplied by (3) the difference in the extent of compliance in firms that are government contractors and those that are not, plus (4) the effect of the debarment penalty on compliance in firms that are not government contractors relative to the change that would have occurred otherwise.

The requirement that a firm comply with the NLRA raises the cost of contracting with the government to firms not in compliance. Since government business constitutes only part of the economy, however, many such firms have a choice. They can continue contracting with the government (incurring the higher cost) or they can avoid the added cost by shifting their business to the nongovernment sector. Thus, the program may do more to change the identity of government contractors than to secure compliance with the U.S. labor laws. A shift of firms for which compliance with the labor laws is most costly from the contractor to the noncontractor sector may even be accompanied by a countervailing shift of noncontractor firms that are in compliance (and hence incur no increased expected cost from the presence of the debarment penalty) toward government contracting. The smaller the share of business constituted by government orders, the more likely is a company to shift its activities away from government contracting rather than comply with the labor law. The problem of adjustments that tend to undermine the objectives of a program is inherent in any policy that alters relative costs because it applies to only part of the labor market.

Structural Changes

Structural changes in the administration of the NLRA that reduce the opportunities to commit unfair labor practices or delay the resolution of unfair practice charges could complement changes in remedial policy. Instant elections, injunctions, and a single forum are among the structural reforms that have been proposed.

INSTANT ELECTIONS. If it is difficult to dissuade the parties from committing unfair labor practices when an opportunity arises, an alternative approach is to remove opportunities for noncompliance. Proposals for "instant elections" for union representation are an example of this approach. An instant election procedure would require a representation election within a few days after a petition for an election is filed with the NLRB.[6] It would eliminate the extended campaigns to persuade workers to vote for or against union representation that are the source of about one-third of unfair labor practice charges in the United States. Instant election procedures are already being used in the Canadian province of British Columbia.

If instant elections eliminated current campaign activities, there could be real savings in resource costs. Whether this would also advance the rights provided by the NLRA depends on whether campaign activities actually do have a coercive effect on worker voting behavior. To the extent that regulated campaign activities do not influence votes, removing the opportunity to initiate such activities is unlikely to advance workers' rights (and conversely). It would, however, reduce the public and private costs of litigation and adjudication.

But would instant elections in fact eliminate the opportunity to commit unfair labor practices? Those employers who believe that many of the activities regulated by the NLRB influence workers' votes will have an incentive to move up or intensify campaign activities to the period before a petition is filed. The strength of this incentive will vary over time as the factors that determine compliance change. When the incentive is strong, however, the actual level of compliance and related litigation may not be altered greatly.

Discussions of instant elections and other structural reforms of the NLRA often overlook the distinction between rights and outcomes and suggest that by reducing opportunities for employers to resist unions, a system of instant elections would contribute to a general increase in union representation. However, it appears that no matter how successful instant elections were in reducing the kind of opposition to unions prohibited under the NLRA, their direct effect on union representation would be limited because more fundamental factors determine the extent of unionization (see chapter 4).

INJUNCTION AGAINST EMPLOYERS. Since the passage of the Taft-Hartley

6. Paul Weiler, "Promises to Keep: Securing Workers' Rights to Self-Organization Under the NLRA," *Harvard Law Review*, vol. 96 (June 1983), pp. 1769–1827.

Act in 1947, section 10.1 of the NLRA has required regional directors of the NLRB to obtain an injunction against certain alleged union violations of the act (for example, secondary boycott activity) as soon as a charge that a union has committed an unfair practice is filed with the regional office. The union's action is halted pending resolution of the charge. When a union files a charge against an employer, however, the action alleged to be in violation of the NLRA is not rectified until the charge is adjudicated.

Given the evidence that delays in adjudication reduce the probability of union success or of reestablishing the status quo in labor relations at the time of a violation (chapter 4), it is hardly surprising that some unions have argued for immediate use of the injunction procedure when unfair practice charges are filed against an employer. Others have argued that only if regulation of labor relations is abandoned can unions avoid this unequal treatment.[7] Although no legislative proposal that incorporated this remedial change has passed Congress, the reform seems desirable because it would remove an important source of damage associated with violations of U.S. labor relations laws. Again, however, it is not clear that the move to better protect the rights guaranteed under the NLRA would have a substantial impact on the extent of the labor force represented by unions.

SINGLE FORUM. Given the apparent effect of delays in adjudication on labor relations outcomes (chapter 4), more rapid enforcement may be a substitute for stronger remedies in achieving greater compliance.[8] Enjoining actions pending resolution of unfair practice charges is consistent with this view. Another suggestion is to have one master forum for hearing all cases relating to violations of laws pertaining to the employment relationship—including violations handled by the Equal Employment Opportunity Commission, the Occupational Safety and Health Administration, and other regulatory agencies. This would create an

7. Testimony of Richard L. Trumka, president of the United Mine Workers of America, in *Oversight Hearings on the Subject "Has Labor Law Failed,"* Joint Hearings before the Subcommittee on Labor-Management Relations of the House Committee on Education and Labor and the Manpower and Housing Subcommittee of the House Committee on Government Operations, 98 Cong. 2 sess. (Government Printing Office, 1984), pt. 1, pp. 6–27.

8. This general approach has been suggested by former NLRB chairmen Edward B. Miller, Frank W. McCulloch, and John Fanning. See *Oversight Hearings on the National Labor Relations Board,* Hearings before the Subcommittee on Labor-Management Relations of the House Committee on Education and Labor, 94 Cong. 1 sess. (GPO, 1976), pp. 249–52.

institution similar to European labor courts—adjudicatory bodies that specialize in problems arising out of the employment relationship.

Delays in adjudication under the NLRA occur partly because of congestion, which is related to the volume of litigation and the budgetary resources of the NLRB. Creating a new institution to administer the same basic set of regulatory rules is unlikely to cause the volume of litigation to change unless it changes either the probability of success or the delays associated with adjudication by the NLRB. The former channel would depend on the appointments process. As to the latter, it is not obvious why a new institution would attract a higher level of resources for adjudication than the NLRB and other bodies now receive. Removing adjudication from the NLRB and giving it to the federal court system would not avoid the congestion problem and could make it even greater.

Deregulation of Labor Relations

The most radical change of direction for U.S. labor policy would be a partial or total deregulation of labor relations in the United States by the repeal, in part or in whole, of the National Labor Relations Act. Deregulation has been advocated by three groups with very different objectives and beliefs about the role of unions and collective bargaining in society and about the effects of the law on labor relations outcomes. For those who believe that the main effect of the NLRA is to facilitate the monopolization of labor markets, deregulation would restore competition and the benefits that come with it to these markets. On the other hand, for labor leaders with rather different conclusions about the effect of the current NLRA on union strength, repeal of the NLRA (but retention of the Norris-LaGuardia Act, which provides a broad definition of legitimate labor disputes and limits the use of injunctions against union activities) would be a way of advancing the power of unions.[9] Having failed to obtain strengthened remedies and administrative reform in the

9. Labor proponents of deregulation hold that as the law has come to be administered it offers greater protection to employers than to workers. This view reflects in part disagreement with certain lines of decision and in part frustration with the consequences of the long delays involved in adjudicating charges under the act. Tied to this is frustration with the asymmetrical use of injunctions against alleged union violations of the act.

labor law reform bill, which did not survive a Senate filibuster in 1978, unions may now be opting for more radical surgery. Or their deregulation proposal may be a tactical move to achieve an eventual compromise along the lines of the remedial reforms proposed in the 1970s. Finally, some academic observers have proposed partial deregulation to eliminate irrelevant regulatory rules that address activities that do not alter industrial relations outcomes.

Selective Repeal of NLRB Rules

The case for partial deregulation of labor relations rests on the proposition that not all the categories of unfair labor practices and not all the rules that have been developed by the NLRB in interpreting the NLRA actually contribute to the employee rights that are established in the statute. All rule making in this regulatory setting is based on certain assumptions about workers and the behavior of the parties in labor relations, and in cases where the assumptions turn out to be incorrect, the resulting regulations may contribute little or nothing to the objectives of the act.

Rules with no direct impact are not innocuous in their effects on labor relations and the regulatory system, however. Even irrelevant rules can have important resource costs associated with litigation and the adjudication of conflict over the application of those rules. Selective repeal of these rules can reduce or eliminate costs without interfering with the rights guaranteed under the NLRA.

When the parties believe that the rules have a bearing on labor relations outcomes, irrelevant rules encourage additional litigation, and the congestion caused by the additional litigation results in delays in adjudication that interfere with the very rights that the statute seeks to guarantee. One of the most consistent findings in the research on elections and contract negotiations is that unions are less likely to prevail if there are long delays in adjudication. Moreover, the empirical analysis in chapter 5 indicates that delays encourage additional congestion—the number of new unfair practice charges varies positively with delays in adjudication. That is, the tendency of delays to encourage noncompliance among employers is stronger than their tendency to reduce the filing of charges by unions. The NLRB and the congressional oversight committees are not unaware that delays are troublesome. But typically they diagnose the problem as a mechanical one of case processing rather than a substantive one of Board doctrine and rule making. The relation between the Board's rules and congestion in the adjudication system receives little attention.

In two areas the results of research or logical argument support selective deregulation. One is in the rules governing the speech of unions and management during campaigns for union representation. Voters in these elections (as in general political elections) seem to recall little of what either party claims, and what is recalled is often remembered imperfectly. Research is persuasive on the point that the precision that the NLRB seeks to achieve with its "laboratory conditions" standard has little pertinence to the context in which union representation choices are made. Since most of the rules regarding speech were developed over the years by the NLRB in its administrative proceedings, congressional action is not required for this aspect of deregulation. The Board itself can simply abandon unproductive rules.

The second area concerns the statutory duty to bargain that is imposed on both parties. While there are few empirical studies of the impact of the duty, analysis of the potential effects of this provision in chapters 2 and 4 indicates that the independent contribution of this provision of the NLRA to the attainment of rights guaranteed by the act is dubious. The legal requirement to bargain appears to be unlikely to alter outcomes that the existing distribution of power between the parties would produce. Because the duty to bargain is written into the statute, explicit congressional action would be required for its repeal.

Further research, stressing the methodological issues discussed in chapter 4, might well expand the list of rules that might be dropped. The finding that in about half of the violations that occurred unions did not bother to file charges of unfair labor practice indicates that many rules are not viewed as having a material effect on outcomes.[10] Ironically, the NLRB is poorly equipped to do such research, for it is probably the only regulatory agency that is prohibited by statute from examining the economic impact of its rule making and remedial activities or the validity of the behavioral assumptions on which its decisions rest. Since 1940 section 4.a of the act has forbidden the NLRB from employing economists and conducting economic research.[11] By default, evaluative activ-

10. Computed from data used in Julius G. Getman, Stephen B. Goldberg, and Jeanne B. Herman, *Union Representation Elections: Law and Reality* (New York: Russell Sage Foundation, 1976).

11. Section 4.c of the NLRA provides that "nothing in this Act shall be construed

ities have been left to academic and other outside groups, which inevitably have been selective in their research. It seems likely that both the number of rules and some of the uncertainty introduced into the compliance game by reversals of Board doctrine and inconsistent decisions resulting from small changes in the underlying assumptions about behavior at the work place could be eliminated if section 4.a were repealed to allow more systematic internal evaluation.

Repeal of the NLRA

Deregulation through repeal of the National Labor Relations Act would leave the Norris-LaGuardia Act to serve as the legal framework of labor relations. Thus there would continue to be a broad definition of what constitutes a legitimate labor dispute, and labor organizations would be protected from most injunctions against union activities. Advocates of repeal of the NLRA include both those who believe the act has advanced and those who believe that it has thwarted the influence of unions in society. The sole point of agreement among the proponents is that repeal would economize on the private and public resource costs associated with administering labor policy.

Repeal of the NLRA would abolish the statutory protection against unfair labor practices and the rules that have been developed by the NLRB to implement the law. Deregulation would therefore permit employers to do everything that they have done in the past plus more. The consequences of abolishing the statutory provisions depend crucially on how significant the impact of the rules has been on labor relations outcomes. For those rules or unfair practices whose impact has been negligible, deregulation implies little change in outcomes. But to the extent that particular rules and unfair practices influence outcomes, deregulation would permit some expansion in employer behavior that might interfere with rights that have been guaranteed in the National Labor Relations Act. However, under the current remedial scheme of the NLRA, there is virtually no economic incentive for employers to comply with rules that they believe would alter the probability of unionization. To the extent that the NLRA has failed to dissuade coercive

---

to authorize the Board to appoint individuals . . . for economic analysis." 61 Stat. 140 (1947). The interesting early political history of the NLRB is reviewed in James A. Gross, *The Reshaping of the National Labor Relations Board: National Labor Policy in Transition, 1937–1947* (Albany: SUNY Press, 1981).

behavior by employers, deregulation obviously would not alter that behavior.

If deregulation would expand the tactics that employers may legally use to resist unions, it also would expand the tactics that unions may use in support of their organizing and collective bargaining goals by removing the NLRA's proscription against secondary boycotts (that is, the immediate injunction against secondary activity by unions pending resolution of disputes through the regulatory process). Whether labor would gain a tactical advantage from abolition of this provision depends crucially on whether secondary boycott activity is likely to be immune from other legal action.

Repeal of the NLRA is likely to be accompanied by an increased level of work stoppages. With removal of the representation election procedures administered by the NLRB, unions would increasingly have to use force to obtain recognition in a deregulated environment. (One of the clearest effects of the NLRA originally was the virtual disappearance of strikes over recognition following the Supreme Court's ruling on its constitutionality.) In addition, deregulation might provide an incentive for more lockouts by employers, since there would no longer be a legal barrier to hiring permanent replacements for employees who have been locked out.

Removal of the current union representation procedures also has implications for bargaining unit determination. Since the determination of an appropriate bargaining unit would no longer be made by a regulatory agency, some meaning might be restored to the AFL-CIO's traditional constitutional power to award jurisdiction. In addition, unions might in some instances seek recognition for smaller units than the NLRB might have permitted. This, plus removal of the exclusive representation feature of the NLRA, would raise the likelihood that some businesses might face a multiplicity of unions (as in European countries, where the concept of exclusive representation is not a part of labor relations law). Indeed, it might be more difficult for employers to avoid some degree of unionization in a labor relations system without the twin features of exclusive jurisdiction and majority rule that are virtually unique to the NLRA.

It is difficult to predict the impact of these or other aspects of deregulation without considering the possible development of legislative substitutes for the NLRA. For example, labor would only gain a tactical advantage from the removal of the NLRA proscription against secondary boycotts if such activity remained immune from other legal action. Interestingly, both before and after the passage of the National Labor Relations Act in 1935, the most common application of antitrust law to labor unions was in controlling secondary boycotts by unions. (In contrast, the courts generally found no antitrust violation in the efforts of unions to organize an entire industry.) With respect to secondary boycotts, repeal of the NLRA could result in an increase in antitrust action against unions rather than a broader scope of tactical freedom.

Another form of legislative substitution would occur at the state level. With fewer situations preempted by federal law, state labor relations legislation, much of it modeled on the NLRA, would play a larger role. Finally, deregulation could increase the demand for legislation providing employment guarantees now covered by collective bargaining and union contracts—for example, requiring that discharges meet a "just cause" rather than an "at will" standard. Again, the distinction between the provision of rights and the provision of union representation is crucial. The very fact that workers would no longer have to look to unions for protection now provided by union contract might further reduce the demand for union representation.

The Compliance Calculus of an Employer

EVIDENCE reported in chapter 5 indicates that some employers apparently comply with the National Labor Relations Act automatically, irrespective of the economic consequences of doing so. Other employers, however, make strategic choices between two kinds of labor relations behavior, on the basis of economic incentives. One type of behavior, B_l, is clearly legal. The other, B_u, is of uncertain legality and may be challenged by a union or individual worker filing an unfair labor practice charge. Strategic employers choose the behavior that will minimize their expected labor costs. A profit-maximizing employer is induced to consider B_u because if unchallenged, the labor costs from such behavior are lower (profits are higher) than from B_l. That is, labor costs are wL if B_l is chosen, and vL if B_u is chosen, where w, the cost per unit of labor input associated with legal behavior, exceeds v, the cost per unit of labor associated with behavior of uncertain legality, and L is labor input.

There is a probability, a, that a strategic employer will choose B_u; a probability, b, that a union will challenge the employer's behavior by filing an unfair labor practice charge; and a further probability, q, that the National Labor Relations Board will sustain the charge. If all this occurs, the employer will be forced to pay the labor costs associated with certain compliance, wL. If punitive damages were permitted, the employer would incur a fine, F, in addition to the compensatory damages. The expected labor costs, C, for a strategic employer, E, are therefore

$$(1)\, E(C) = a\{b[q(wL + F) + (1 - q)(vL) + c] + (1 - b)(vL)\} + (1 - a)(wL).$$

The last term on the right-hand side of this expression captures the labor costs of certain compliance weighted by the probability that the employer will choose that option. The remainder of the expression describes the expected costs of choosing B_u. The long term in square brackets describes the expected costs of B_u if the union chooses to file a charge with the NLRB. Even if the charge is rejected by the Board (with probability $1-q$), the gain in lower labor costs is to some extent offset by the litigation costs, c.

The marginal benefit (in terms of lower expected labor costs) to the employer, MB^e, from choosing B_u is simply the derivative of equation 1 with respect to a, or

(2) $$MB^e = b\{q[(w-v)L + F] + c\} + (v-w)L.$$

The employer will take whatever action reduces labor costs, and since $v-w$ is negative, it is clear that an employer will choose B_u if $(w-v)L > b\{q[(w-v)L + F] + c\}$. A key aspect of the interaction between an employer and a union is b, the likelihood that the union will file an unfair labor practice charge. An employer will be indifferent between compliance and noncompliance when equation 2 equals zero (that is, the marginal benefit of choosing B_u is zero). Therefore, the particular value of b that sets equation 2 equal to zero is a critical or threshold response in terms of the employer's choice. Call this threshold value b'. If the probability that a union will file a charge exceeds b', the expected costs will be minimized by choosing safe behavior, B_l, rather than choosing B_u and running the risk of detection and the penalties that detection entails. If the probability is less than b', expected costs will be minimized by adopting B_u.

The threshold response is defined as

(3) $$b' = (w-v)L/\{q[(w-v)L + F] + c\}.$$

Punitive fines are not permitted under the NLRA, so $F = 0$. Therefore, it is clear that if $q < 1$ (that is, success with the NLRB is not guaranteed), or c is small, b' could easily reach unity and there would be no probability of facing an unfair labor practice charge, b, that would induce a strategic employer to choose certain compliance, B_l. The implications of this result are discussed in chapter 5.

It is noted in chapter 5 that because the NLRB must process all cases that are filed with it and because its operating budget is not automatically altered with variations in its caseload, the filing of additional unfair labor practice charges can at times produce congestion effects that result in delays in adjudication. Evidence reviewed in chapter 4 indicates that such delays tend to diminish the gains that unions get from even favorable NLRB rulings. If D represents the time that it takes to investigate and adjudicate a charge, the union's payoff from a favorable ruling becomes $[(w/D) - v]L$. This merely reinforces the point made in discussing the implications of equation 3. The threshold response now becomes b'', or

(4) $b'' = (w - v)L/(q\{[(w/D) - v]L + F\} + c).$

With $F = 0$, employers are even less likely to choose certain compliance as D increases. In addition, when congestion effects are operative, unions have an incentive to file fewer charges to keep D low.

Index

Administration, NLRA: NLRB Office of General Counsel role, 18, 19; proposed reforms, 4, 107–10
AFL-CIO, study of union representation elections, 58
Alleluia Cushions, Co., 18n
American Ship Building Co. v. *NLRB*, 17n
Apcar, Leonard M., 4n, 27n
Ashenfelter, Orley, 55n
Atleson, James B., 4n, 10n

Bain, George Sayers, 8n
Becker, Gary S., 74n, 78n, 82n, 104n
Belleville Employing Printers, 32n
Bernstein, Irving, 27n
Block, Richard N., 58n
Bok, Derek C., 4n, 13n, 60n
Brett, Jeanne M., 60n
Bruno, Michael, 97n

Calmfors, Lars, 98n
Canada: labor relations policy, 38, 49, 72; unfair labor practice charges, 39–41, 42
Chaney, Warren, 21n
Charleston Transit Co., 32n
Clark, Kim B., 86n
Collective bargaining, 1; centralized versus decentralized, 97–99; classification of issues, 15; contract negotiations, 63–65; criticism of policies, 3–4; duty to engage in good faith, 3, 14–16, 23, 63, 65; mandatory versus voluntary issues, 65–66; NLRA efforts to encourage, 104–05; remedial orders to initiate, 21; unit, 10, 12, 87, 114
Common law, labor relations regulations and, 8, 9
Company unions, 9, 21
Competition: deregulation effect on labor market, 103; NLRA effect, 3; nonunion firm, 99
Compliance, NLRA, 1–2; adjudication delays and, 91, 94, 95, 117–18; benefit-cost considerations, 80–81; decline, 76; elec-

tion unit size and, 87; employer's strategic approach, 77–83; labor cost effect, 85–87, 94, 95, 116–17; measures, 75–76; probability of litigation success and, 87–89; regulatory incentives influencing, 84, 95, 97, 100; shifts in employer attitudes and, 101; stages in procedure for, 74–75; union decisions, 83–84. *See also* Noncompliance, NLRA
Conair Corp., 13n
Congress, intentions in NLRA enactment, 9, 14, 15, 63, 103
Cooke, William N., 57n, 64n
Cooper, Laura, 58n
Cornell University, 30n
Cox, Archibald, 16n
Craver, Charles B., 21n

Dennis, Barbara D., 16n, 58n, 76n, 87n, 99n
Deregulation, labor relations: arguments for and against, 110–11; labor versus management support, 27; NLRA repeal, 113–14; partial, 4, 111–13; public policy choice, 103; substitute legislation, 114–15
Dickens, William T., 4n, 53, 57n, 58n, 61, 62
Dotson, Donald L., 30n, 31n
Drotning, John, 57n
Duncan, Greg J., 55n

East Oakland Community Health Alliance, Inc., 30n
Ehrenberg, Ronald G., 55n
Elections. *See* Union representation elections
Emergency dispute procedures, 2, 17n
Enforcement, NLRA, 2; initiation of proceedings, 73, 74; percent of NLRB activities, 22; procedures, 18–20; proposal for more rapid, 109; secondary boycotts, 17; success probability, 88
Epstein, Richard A., 3n, 8n